A Catechism of Catholic
Social Teaching

Gerald Darring

Sheed & Ward

Sheed & Ward™ is a service of National Catholic Reporter Publishing Company, Inc.

Library of Congress Catalog Card Number: 87-62380

ISBN:1-55612-084-2

Published by: Sheed & Ward
            115 E. Armour Blvd. P.O. Box 414292
            Kansas City, MO 64141-4292

To order, call: (800) 333-7373

Contents

Introduction iv

I
General Principles

1. Social Justice (Questions 1-44) 1

2. Economic Justice (45-92) 25

3. Political Justice (93-116) 55

II
Specific Areas of Social Justice

4. Discrimination (117-125) 68

   a. Racial Discrimination (126-134) 73

   b. Discrimination Against Women (135-140) 78

   c. Discrimination Against the Aged (141-143) 81

   d. Discrimination Against the Handicapped (144-147) . . . 83

   e. Anti-Semitism (148-149) 85

5. War and Peace (150-168) 87

6. Capital Punishment (169-178) 100

7. Abortion (179-184) 106

Bibliography 110

Index of Sources 111

Index of Topics 115

Introduction

In the century following the promulgation of Leo XIII's encyclical "On the Condition of Workers" ("Rerum Novarum") the Catholic Church has produced a significant volume of teachings on the major social issues of our time. This book is an attempt to synthesize the main outlines of that teaching in a compact, accessible form.

The format is that of question and answer, the old catechism format. Each question is answered with a direct quote from an official document of the Church: a conciliar decree, a papal encyclical, a synodal document, or a pastoral letter from the national conference of bishops. Official statements are used exclusively, not because they are necessarily the best in every case but because they represent official Catholic viewpoints. Only pastoral letters by the bishops of the United States are quoted because this work is intended for an American audience.

There are several advantages to the catechism format. First, the basic elements of Catholic social teaching are presented in short, concise passages that enable the reader to focus on one concept at a time. A whole century of social thought is condensed here, and there are quotes from three documents of Vatican II, seventeen papal documents, a synodal decree, and twenty-nine pastoral letters and statements of the American bishops. A lot of background and explanation is missing, but the main elements are there, neatly arranged.

Second, the questions guide the reader through the material. They point the way, focusing the reader's attention and providing an outline. Not only is there the overall outline: social justice, economic justice, political justice, and specific areas of social justice (discrimination, war and peace, capital punishment, abortion). There is also a system of grouping questions within these divisions, as for example in questions 28-33 (the Church and social justice), 61-64 (the preferential option for the poor), 69-73 (work), and 81-83 (unemployment).

Finally, for those who are using the catechism in connection with a course, the questions provide a handy study guide.

But there are disadvantages as well to the catechism format. One serious disadvantage which concerns me greatly is the inability of a catechism like this to provide the reader with a sense of the development of Catholic thought. Reading through the catechism, one might easily get the impression that the church has always been aware of these things, that Leo XIII and Paul VI are of the same piece. Catholic social thought has come a long way in the last century, and the reader is cautioned not to conclude that the church's social teaching is a static doctrine, fixed and unchanging. It has evolved and will continue to do so.

A second disadvantage to the catechism format is the impression of dogmatism it gives. There is a natural tendency to view each question as having one, and only one, correct answer. Even assuming that the answer is correct, who is to say that it will not be improved upon in the future? But are all these answers 'correct'? The church of the Middle Ages and the post-Tridentine church would not have been happy with some of these answers. Would a catechism of the twenty-second century use all of these answers, unchanged? I doubt it. And then, of course, there is the example of question 59 of this catechism, which has two distinct answers for the same question. Which of them is 'the' answer?

There is a great distance between the foundational principle stated in question 2 and the policy position taken in question 123. The reader should be able to make such distinctions as he works his way through the catechism; if he is a student, he should be guided by his instructor to make such distinctions.

The reader should also be aware of the relative weight attached to church documents. A conciliar statement is acknowledged to have more weight than a statement in an encyclical, while the latter is of greater significance than a pastoral letter from the conference of bishops. Moreover, an encyclical has more weight than a papal speech in Yankee Stadium, and a pastoral letter from the bishops is regarded as more weighty than a statement by a committee of the bishops' conference. This is not to take away from any of the statements used in this catechism; it is simply a word of caution to the reader who wants to use the material correctly.

A third disadvantage to the catechism format is its potential abuse by teachers who only know how to present material for rote memorization. A catechism plays right into their hands: students, they will say, memorize the answers to the next ten questions for tomorrow. Nothing could be farther from my intention in preparing this book. The purpose of this book is to give the reader, including the student, the opportunity to encounter Catholic social teaching; it is not to turn him against it.

I wish that all people of good will would catch the spirit of Catholic social teaching, a spirit of respect, love, forgiveness, redemption. In a world ravaged by war, my church clamors for peace. In a world torn apart by divisions of all sorts, my church tries to bring people together, to reconcile them. In a world of oppression, violence, torture, crime, persecution, and injustice, my church speaks of freedom, nonviolence, order, and respect for rights. It is not the only voice speaking of these things, but it is a clear and powerful voice. It is not a radical, avant-garde voice, but it carries with it the authority of a worldwide community of faith and two thousand years of experience.

How faithful is this catechism to the voice of the Catholic Church? Since all of the answers are given in the form of direct quotes from official church documents, one might say that this work is right on the mark, faithfully outlining Catholic social teaching. On the other hand, who chose these passages? Who decided that these and not other passages would be included? Who formulated the questions? Who placed the questions and answers in the order in which they appear. I, of course, am responsible for all of these decisions, and it would be foolish on everyone's part to deny any subjective element in those decisions. I alone must be held accountable for the choice of passages, the wording of the questions, and the ordering of the text, and I hope that the knowledgeable reader will determine that I made not the only possible choices but certainly good choices in the true spirit of authentic Catholic social teaching.

This has been for me a labor of love. I am seldom as much at home as when I am teaching Catholic social thought. I try with all my energy to pass that feeling on to my students. The catechism has been a great support in my efforts. It is not a textbook, of course, but it is a unique reference work, available for easy use in covering the material in the main text. My principal use of the catechism in the classroom is as the basis for discussion. The reflections following each text will hopefully provide a useful guide in conducting discussions and help the student to confront the main elements of the passage under consideration.

I dedicate this book to my wife Dolores, who has taught me much of what I know about truth, beauty, love, forgiveness, and respect, that is to say, all the things that go to make up justice. She has been a wonderful answer to my question.

I

General Principles

1

Social Justice.

1. How does Catholic thought view social justice?

In Catholic thought, social justice is not merely a secular or humanitarian matter. Social justice is a reflection of God's essential respect and concern for each person and an effort to protect the essential human freedom necessary for each person to achieve his or her destiny as a child of God.

U.S. Bishops, To Do the Work of Justice (1978) 8.

Reflections on the Catholic view of social justice:

a) What is God's attitude toward you and me?
b) Why is human freedom necessary?
c) Do you agree that human freedom needs protection? Why?

2. What are the three dimensions of basic justice?

Catholic social teaching, like much philosophical reflection, distinguishes three dimensions of basic justice: commutative justice, distributive justice, and social justice. Commutative justice calls for fundamental fairness in all agreements and exchanges between individuals or private social groups.... Distributive justice requires that the allocation of income, wealth, and power in society be evaluated in light of its effects on persons whose basic material needs are unmet.... Social justice implies that persons have an obligation to be active and productive participants in the life of society and that society has a duty to enable them to participate in this way.

U.S. Bishops, Economic Justice for All (1986) 68-71.

Reflections on the three dimensions of basic justice.

a) Describe each type of justice in your own words.
b) Give an example of each type of justice at work.
c) Give an example of a violation of each type of justice.

3. What principle is at the foundation of human society?

Any human society, if it is to be well-ordered and productive, must lay down as a foundation this principle: that every human being is a person; his nature is endowed with intelligence and free will. By virtue of this, he has rights and duties of his own, flowing directly and simultaneously from his very nature, which are therefore universal, inviolable, and inalienable. If we look upon the dignity of the human person in the light of divinely revealed truth, we cannot help but esteem it far more highly; for men are redeemed by the blood of Jesus Christ, they are by grace the children and friends of God and heirs of eternal glory.

Pope John XXIII, Peace on Earth (1963) 9-10.

Reflections on the foundational principle of human society.

a) Would the following people agree or disagree with the proposition that "every human being is a person"?
• A prison guard who tortures a suspect;
• A Nazi worker who turns on the gas killing a roomful of Jews;
• A slaveowner who beats a slave trying to escape;
• A doctor who routinely performs abortions;
• A member of a death squad in El Salvador.
b) Do you believe that every single member of the human race has intelligence and free will?
c) What does it mean to say that rights and duties are universal?
d) What does it mean to say that rights and duties are inviolable?
e) What does it mean to say that rights and duties are inalienable?
f) Do Christians believe that everyone, or just some people, are redeemed by the blood of Jesus Christ?

4. In what does the common welfare of society consist?

The common welfare of society consists in the entirety of those conditions of social life under which men enjoy the possibility of achieving their own perfection in a certain fullness of measure and also with some relative ease. Hence this welfare consists chiefly in the protection of the rights, and in the performance of the duties, of the human person.

Vatican II, Declaration on Religious Freedom (1965) 6.

Reflections on the common welfare of society.

a) This statement says that society is well provided for when rights are protected and duties are performed. Do you agree with this description of the common welfare?

b) Why is a society unjust if within it rights are protected but duties are not performed?

c) Why is a society unjust if within it duties are performed but rights are not protected?

d) Do you think Soviet society is more like the one described in "b" or more like the one in "c"?

e) Do you think American society is more like the one described in "b" or more like the one in "c"?

5. What is at the center of all Catholic social teaching?

At the center of all Catholic social teaching are the transcendence of God and the dignity of the human person. The human person is the clearest reflection of God's presence in the world; all of the Church's work in pursuit of both justice and peace is designed to protect and promote the dignity of every person. For each person not only reflects God, but is the expression of God's creative work and the meaning of Christ's redemptive ministry.

U. S. Bishops, The Challenge of Peace (1983) 15.

Reflections on the center of Catholic social teaching.

a) The "transcendence of God" refers to God's otherness, his being beyond all human and created reality. What does that have to do with social justice?

b) Do you agree with the bishops that you reflect God's presence in the world? What does that mean?

c) How is the church protecting and promoting the dignity of every person when it

• seeks to remove racism from society?

• tries to bring the arms race to an end?

• speaks out against the practice of abortion?

• organizes Latin American poor people to work toward improvement of their lot?

• works for the removal of all forms of political oppression?

6. What is the cardinal point of Catholic teaching regarding social life and relationships of men?

> What the Catholic Church teaches and declares regarding the social life and relationships of men is beyond question for all time valid. The cardinal point of this teaching is that individual men are necessarily the foundation, cause, and end of all social institutions.
>
> *Pope John XXIII, On Christianity and Social Progress (1961) 218-19.*

Reflections on the cardinal point of Catholic social teaching.

a) Do you think that every political, economic, and social system in the world is based on a recognition of this "cardinal point"?

b) What does it mean to say that individual people are the foundation of all social institutions?

c) What does it mean to say that individual people are the cause of all social institutions?

d) What does it mean to say that individual people are the end of all social institutions?

7. What is the norm of human activity?

> The norm of human activity is this: that in accord with the divine plan and will, it should harmonize with the genuine good of the human race, and allow men as individuals and as members of society to pursue their total vocation and fulfill it.
>
> *Vatican II, Church in the Modern World (1965) 35.*

Reflections on the norm of human activity.

a) Wouldn't everyone always say that what he is doing is for the genuine good of the human race? Didn't the Nazis think that when they murdered millions of Jews? Don't South African white supporters of apartheid think that what they are doing is in harmony with the genuine good of the human race? Well, then, what is the problem?

b) What is the "total vocation" of individual men and women?

c) What is the "total vocation" of society?

8. Which must yield to the other: the social order or the good of the person?

The social order and its development must constantly yield to the good of the person, since the order of things must be subordinate to the order of persons and not the other way around, as the Lord suggested when he said that the Sabbath was made for man and not man for the Sabbath.

Vatican II, Church in the Modern World (1965) 26.

Reflections on the priority of the good of the person.

a) Can you think of a concrete example showing the necessity for giving priority to the person over the social order?

b) Would you want to live in a society in which this principle is regularly violated? Why?

9. What are some of the most important and universally recognized human rights?

Permit me to enumerate some of the most important human rights that are universally recognized: the right to life, liberty and security of person; the right to food, clothing, housing, sufficient health care, rest and leisure; the right to freedom of expression, education and culture; the right to freedom of thought, conscience and religion; and the right to manifest one's religion either individually or in community, in public or in private; the right to choose a state of life, to found a family and to enjoy all conditions necessary for family life; the right to property and work, to adequate working conditions and a just wage; the right of assembly and association; the right to freedom of movement, to internal and external migration; the right to nationality and residence; the right to political participation and the right to participate in the free choice of the political system of the people to which one belongs.

Pope John Paul II, Address at the United Nations (1979) 13.

Reflections on basic human rights.

a) Which of the above rights are political?
b) Which of the above rights are economic?
c) Which of the above rights are social or cultural?
d) How much are each of these rights respected in American society?

10. How is the right to life violated in our day?

The right to life... is basic and inalienable. It is grievously violated in our day by abortion and euthanasia, by widespread torture, by acts of violence against innocent parties, and by the scourge of war. The arms race is an insanity which burdens the world and creates the conditions for even more massive destruction of life.

Pope Paul VI, Message Issued in Union with the Synod of Bishops (1974).

Reflections on violations of the right to life.

a) Show how each of the following violates the right to life:
- abortion
- euthanasia
- torture
- acts of violence against innocent parties
- war
- the arms race.

b) Do you agree with the description of the arms race as an "insanity"? Why?

11. How are individuals and groups to exercise their rights?

In the exercise of their rights, individual men and social groups are bound by the moral law to have respect both for the rights of others and for their own duties toward others and for the common welfare of all.

Vatican II, Declaration on Religious Freedom (1965) 7.

Reflections on exercising individual and group rights.

a) Why is it so important for me to respect the rights of others in the process of exercising my rights?

b) Give some examples of "duties toward others."

12. How must social institutions be ordered?

Justice demands that social institutions be ordered in a way that guarantees all persons the ability to participate actively in the economic, political, and cultural life of society.

U.S. Bishops, Economic Justice for All (1986) 78.

Reflections on the ordering of social institutions.

a) Give examples of active participation in economic life.

b) Give examples of active participation in political life.

c) Give examples of active participation in cultural life.

d) Do you agree that active participation in each of these areas of life should be GUARANTEED ALL PERSONS?

13. What is required of us besides the acknowledgement of each other's rights and duties?

A well-ordered human society requires that men recognize and observe their mutual rights and duties. It also demands that each contribute generously to the establishment of a civic order in which rights and duties are progressively more sincerely and effectively acknowledged and fulfilled. It is not enough, for example, to acknowledge and respect every man's right to the means of subsistence. One must also strive to insure that he actually has enough in the way of food and nourishment.

Pope John XXIII, Peace on Earth (1963) 31-32.

Reflections on going beyond the acknowledgement of rights and duties.

a) Restate in one sentence the answer to question 13.

b) Why is the word "strive" important in the last sentence?

c) Taking care of myself uses up a considerable amount of my time and energy. Explain why justice requires me to be concerned with the survival situation of others.

14. What causes social disturbances?

The disturbances which so frequently occur in the social order result in part from the natural tensions of economic, political, and social forms. But at a deeper level they flow from man's pride and selfishness, which contaminate even the social sphere.

Vatican II, Church in the Modern World (1965) 25.

Reflections on the causes of social disturbances.

a) Give some examples of the "natural tensions" which often disturb the social order.
b) The statement makes a connection between pride and what happens in society. Explain what that connection is and give a couple of examples (either real or fictitious).

15. How does Jesus' command to love one's neighbor relate to social justice?

Christians believe that Jesus' commandment to love one's neighbor should extend beyond individual relationships to infuse and transform all human relationships from the family to the entire human community. Jesus came to 'bring good news to the poor, to proclaim liberty to captives, new sight to the blind and to set the downtrodden free' (Lk 4:18). He called us to feed the hungry, clothe the naked, care for the sick and afflicted, and to comfort the victims of injustice (Mt 25). His example and words require individual acts of charity and concern from each of us. Yet they also require understanding and action upon the broader dimensions of poverty, hunger, and injustice which necessarily involve the institutions and structures of economy, society, and politics.

U.S. Bishops, Political Responsibility (Feb 1976) 6.

Reflections on social justice and the command to love one's neighbor.

a) When you think of the commandment to love your neighbor, do you usually think only of individual relationships or do you think of everyone "from the family to the entire human community"? Why?

b) What are some things we can do to satisfy the requirement of "understanding" mentioned in the statement?

c) What are some things we can do to satisfy the requirement of "action" mentioned in the statement?

d) Give some examples of the "institutions and structures" mentioned in the statement.

16. What two things must we do to help, liberate, and heal the world?

Because we believe in the dignity of the person, we must embrace every chance to help and to liberate, to heal the wounded world as Jesus taught us. Our hands must be the strong but gentle hands of Christ, reaching out in mercy and justice, touching individual persons, but also touching the social conditions that hinder the wholeness which is God's desire for humanity.

U.S. Bishops, Health and Health Care (1981) 13.

Reflections on things we must do for the world.

a) Give two examples of reaching out in mercy and justice and touching individual persons.

b) Give two examples of reaching out in mercy and justice and touching social conditions.

c) Do you accept the bishops' assertion that we should be concerned with both individual persons and social conditions? Why?

17. What is the principle of subsidiarity?

It is a fundamental principle of social philosophy, fixed and unchangeable, that one should not withdraw from individuals and commit to the community what they can accomplish by their own enterprise and industry. So, too, it is an injustice and at the same time a grave evil and a disturbance of right order, to transfer to the larger and higher collectivity functions which can be performed and provided for by lesser and subordinate bodies. Inasmuch as every social activity should, by its very nature, prove a help to members of the body social, it should never destroy or absorb them.

> *Pope Pius XI, On Reconstructing the Social Order (1931)* 79.

Reflections on the principle of subsidiarity.

a) Restate the principle of subsidiarity in one sentence.
b) Give an example of this principle in operation.
c) Give an example of a violation of this principle.

18. Why do we have to be concerned with injustices we have not caused?

The absence of personal fault for an evil does not absolve one of all responsibility. We must seek to resist and undo injustices we have not caused, lest we become bystanders who tacitly endorse evil and so share in guilt for it.

> *U.S. Bishops, To Live in Christ Jesus (1976) 71.*

Reflections on concern for injustices we have not caused.

a) Restate the answer to question 18 briefly in your own words.
b) Why does being a bystander make me guilty for the evil?
c) Give an example of how this principle works.

19. Who are the most common victims of social injustice?

Most often it is the weak and unfortunate, the poor, the aged, the young, minorities and women who are forced to bear injustice.

> *U.S. Bishops, Community and Crime (1978) 19.*

Reflections on victims of social injustice.

a) Do you agree or disagree with this statement? Give an example or two supporting your position.

b) Why do you think the people listed here are more subject to injustice that the rest of us?

20. What is the ultimate injustice?

The ultimate injustice is for a person or group to be actively treated or passively abandoned as if they were nonmembers of the human race. To treat people this way is effectively to say that they simply do not count as human beings.

U.S. Bishops, Economic Justice for All (1986) 77.

Reflections on the ultimate injustice.

a) How many concrete examples of "the ultimate injustice" can you think of?
b) Is it possible for anyone to be so evil that he/she does not count as a human being?

21. How does our struggle to overcome social injustice relate to our conflict with communism?

Today the world watches us anxiously, as it reads of racial struggles and tensions and learns about poverty in an affluent society. If men elsewhere become disillusioned with our democracy, they are offered the choice of another powerful system which also promises equality, but at the sacrifice of basic freedoms.

U.S. Bishops, Race Relations and Poverty (1966) 24.

Reflections on social justice and our conflict with communism.

a) According to this statement, why would a people ever choose communism when they have the chance to choose democracy?
b) Are the bishops using a scare tactic, or do you think their warning is justified?

22. What should be our attitude toward those who discriminate, oppress, or are otherwise unjust?

We must distinguish between the error (which must always be rejected) and the person in error, who never loses his dignity as a person even though he flounders amid false or inadequate religious ideas. God alone is the judge and the searcher of hearts; he forbids us to pass judgment on the inner guilt of others. The teaching of Christ even demands that we forgive injury, and the precept of love, which is the commandment of the New Law, includes all our enemies.

Vatican II, Church in the Modern World (1965) 28.

Reflections on our attitude toward the unjust.

a) Why is it impossible for someone to lose his dignity as a person?

b) Do you find it hard to believe that someone like Hitler, who had millions of Jews, Poles, gypsies, and others killed, never lost his dignity as a person?

c) Isn't it a bit unrealistic to expect people to forgive someone like Hitler?

d) The Vatican II statement does not say anything about discrimination, oppression, or injustice. Explain the connection between the question and the statement from Vatican II.

23. How important to Catholics is action on behalf of justice?

Action on behalf of justice and participation in the transformation of the world fully appear to us as a constitutive dimension of the preaching of the Gospel, or, in other words, of the Church's mission for the redemption of the human race and its liberation from every oppressive situation.

Synod of Bishops, Justice in the World (1971) 6.

The quest for human freedom is not optional for Catholics, nor is it a small part of the Church's mission. Participation in the struggle for freedom and justice is a duty for each one of us, as it is a central element of the Church's mission of redemption

and liberation.
U.S. Bishops, The Eucharist and the Hungers of the Human Family (1975) 12.

Reflections on the importance of action on behalf of justice.

a) The synod statement says that working for a just world is part of preaching the Gospel, in other words, if you want to tell people about Jesus Christ, part of your message has to be your action on behalf of a just world. Do you agree or disagree? Why?

b) The second statement says that Catholics have no choice but to work for freedom and justice. Do you agree or disagree? Why?

c) Both statements mention the Church's mission. Describe briefly what you think is the Church's mission.

24. Why can't we be content with a merely individualistic morality?

Profound and rapid changes make it particularly urgent that no one, ignoring the trend of events or drugged by laziness, content himself with a merely individualistic morality. It grows increasingly true that the obligations of justice and love are fulfilled only if each person, contributing to the common good, according to his own abilities and the needs of others, also promotes and assists the public and private institutions dedicated to bettering the conditions of human life.
Vatican II, Church in the Modern World (1965) 30.

Reflections on individualistic morality.

a) Describe what you think is meant in this statement by "individualistic morality." Does the statement say it is bad or inadequate? Why?

b) Give an example of an institution that is "dedicated to bettering the conditions of human life," and tell how you can promote and assist it.

25. Why do Jesus' followers work for just laws, policies, and social structures?

As followers of Jesus we are called to express love of neighbor in deeds which help others realize their human potential. This, too, has consequences for the structures of society. Law and public policy do not substitute for the personal acts by which we express love of neighbor; but love of neighbor impels us to work for laws, policies, and social structures which foster human goods in the lives of all persons.

U.S. Bishops, To Live in Christ Jesus (1976) 62.

Reflections on the work for justice as followers of Jesus.

a) The statement mentions "the structures of society" and "social structures." Describe what is meant by these structures.

b) What do these structures have to do with being followers of Jesus?

c) Do you agree that our love for neighbor has to be expressed both privately, through personal acts, and publicly through "work for laws, policies, and social structures"?

26. Will the building of proper social structures suffice to create a just society?

The Church considers it to be undoubtedly important to build up structures which are more human, more just, more respectful of the rights of the person and less oppressive and less enslaving, but she is conscious that the best structures and the most idealized systems soon become inhuman if the inhuman inclinations of the human heart are not made wholesome, if those who live in these structures or who rule them do not undergo a conversion of heart and of outlook.

Pope Paul VI, Evangelization in the Modern World (1975) 36.

Reflections on what is needed to create a just society.

a) Give an example of a structure that would be human, just, and respectful of the rights of the person, and give an example of a structure that would be oppressive and enslaving.

b) Why isn't changing structures good enough? Why do we also have to "undergo a conversion of heart and of outlook"?

27. What is Christ's role in the Christian search for justice?

It is in Christ that the Church finds the central cause for its commitment to justice, and to the struggle for the human rights and dignity of all persons.... It is Christ's word that is the judgment on this world; it is Christ's cross that is the measure of our response; and it is Christ's face that is the composite of all persons, but in a most significant way of today's poor, today's marginal people, today's minorities.

U.S. Bishops, Brothers and Sisters to Us (1979) 10, 23.

Reflections on Christ's role in the search for justice.

a) Describe in your own words the relationship between Christ and our struggle for justice.

28. Where does the Church's social teaching find its source?

The church's social teaching finds its source in sacred scripture, beginning with the Book of Genesis and especially in the Gospel and the writings of the apostles.

Pope John Paul II, On Human Work (1981) 3.

Reflections on the source of the Church's social teaching.

a) Why is it important to be able to trace the church's social teaching back to the Bible?

29. What is the Church's responsibility in the area of social justice?

The Church has the right, indeed the duty, to proclaim justice on the social, national, and international level, and to denounce instances of injustice, when the fundamental rights of man and his very salvation demand it. The Church, indeed, is not alone responsible for justice in the world; however, she has a proper and specific responsibility which is identified with her mission of giving witness before the world of the need for love and justice contained in the gospel message, a witness to be carried out in Church institutions themselves and in the lives of Christians.

Synod of Bishops, Justice in the World (1971) 36.

Reflections on the Church's role in pursuing social justice.

a) The bishops claim that the Church has the right to speak out on behalf of justice. Do you agree?
b) The bishops claim that the Church has the right to condemn injustice wherever they find it. Do you agree?
c) What does it mean to say that, as part of its social responsibility, the Church should give witness to justice in its institutions?
d) What does it mean to say that, as part of its social responsibility, the Church should give witness to justice in the lives of its members?

30. What is the basis for the Church's influence on the human community?

Christ, to be sure, gave his Church no proper mission in the political, economic, or social order. The purpose which He set before her is a religious one. But out of this religious mission itself come a function, a light, and an energy which can serve to structure and consolidate the human community according to the divine law.

Vatican II, Church in the Modern World (1965) 42.

Reflections on the basis for the Church's influence.

a) Describe in your own words the "religious" mission of the Church.
b) What does this mission have to do with the struggle for social justice?

31. What two functions does the Church wish to assume in the social sphere?

In the social sphere, the Church has always wished to assume a double function: first, to enlighten minds in order to assist them to discover the truth and to find the right path to follow amid the different teachings that call for their attention; and second, to take part in action and to spread, with a real care for service and effectiveness, the energies of the Gospel.

Pope Paul VI, A Call to Action (1971) 48.

Reflections on the two functions of the Church in the social sphere.

a) Describe in your own words the two functions mentioned in this statement.
b) Do you agree that these are legitimate functions of the Church in society? Why?

32. What is the Church's relationship to particular economic, political, or social systems?

The church is not bound to any particular economic, political, or social system; it has lived with many forms of economic and social organization and will continue to do so, evaluating each according to moral and ethical principles: What is the impact of the system on people? Does it support or threaten human dignity?

U.S. Bishops, Economic Justice for All (1986) 130.

Reflections on the Church and economic, political, and social systems.

a) Don't we sometimes act as though the Catholic Church is tied to the American political system? What do you think is the proper relationship between being a Catholic and being an American?
b) Give two examples, one of an economic system that has a positive impact on people and one of an economic system that has a negative impact on people.
c) Do the same with political systems.
d) Do the same with social systems.

33. What is the Church's responsibility in the area of human rights?

The Church's responsibility in the area of human rights includes two complementary pastoral actions: the affirmation and promotion of human rights and the denunciation and condemnation of violations of these rights. In addition, it is the Church's role to call attention to the moral and religious dimensions of secular issues, to keep alive the values of the Gospel as a norm for social and political life, and to point out the demands of the Christian faith for a just transformation of society. Such a ministry on the part of every Christian and the Church inevitably involves political consequences and touches upon public affairs.

> *U.S. Bishops, Political Responsibility (Feb 1976) 8.*

Reflections on the Church and human rights.

a) Tell whether you think each of the following is a legitimate responsibility of the Church:
• to speak and teach about human rights
• to condemn situations in which human rights are violated
• to study current affairs and point out any moral or religious aspects which should be taken into account
• to teach the values of the Gospel as a guide for life in society
• to help Christians understand how their faith obliges them to work for a just society
b) Show what the Church can do to perform each of these functions.

34. What is the principle of religious freedom?

This Vatican Synod declares that the human person has a right to religious freedom. This freedom means that all men are to be immune from coercion on the part of individuals or of social groups and of any human power, in such wise that in matters religious no one is to be forced to act in a manner contrary to his own beliefs.

> *Vatican II, Declaration on Religious Freedom (1965) 2.*

Reflections on the principle of religious freedom.

a) Describe what you understand by religious freedom.

b) Why do you suppose there is, and always has been, resistance to religious freedom? Is religion all that dangerous?

c) Have you ever felt "forced to act in a manner contrary to your own beliefs"? If so, describe your feelings.

35. Why should the free exercise of religion be permitted in society?

The social nature of man itself requires that he should give external expression to his internal acts of religion; that he should participate with others in matters religious; that he should profess his religion in community. Injury, therefore, is done to the human person and to the very order established by God for human life, if the free exercise of religion is denied in society when the just requirements of public order do not so require.

Vatican II, Declaration on Religious Freedom (1965) 3.

Reflections on the free exercise of religion.

a) Answer the question briefly in your own words.

b) What kind of "injury" is done to the person who is not allowed the free exercise of religion?

36. What does the Church see in the poor, the afflicted, and the oppressed?

As a leaven in the world, the Church is called to participate in human affairs and to recognize in the poor, the afflicted, and the oppressed the presence of the Lord summoning the Christian community to action.

U.S. Bishops, Resolution on the Pastoral Concern of the Church for People on the Move (1976) 5.

Reflections on the poor, afflicted, and oppressed.

a) Why is the Church compared to a leaven in the world?

b) According to this statement, what does the Church see in the poor, the afflicted, and the oppressed? Can you relate to that, does it have any meaning to you?

37. Why can't the Church neglect such violations of human rights as racism, poverty, and lack of freedom?

In all its activities the Church must seek to preach and act in ways that lead to greater justice for all people. Its ministry cannot neglect the violations of human rights resulting from racism, poverty, poor housing, inadequate education and health care, widespread apathy and indifference, and a lack of freedom. These realities are fundamentally incompatible with our faith, and the Church is required to oppose them.

U.S. Bishops, Statement on American Indians (1977) 10.

Reflections on the Church and violations of human rights.

a) How does each of the following cause a violation of human rights:
• racism
• poverty
• poor housing
• inadequate education
• inadequate health care
• apathy and indifference
• lack of freedom.

b) According to the statement, why can't the Church neglect these realities?

38. Is the hope in another life a threat to our commitment to social justice?

All too often Christians are faulted with a certain indifference toward earthly projects, as if one could not fully count on us for radical social reform. The charge may be unfair, but the danger is real enough. Our hope in another life must not be allowed to seduce believers into neglecting our task in the present one.

U.S. Bishops, Pastoral Letter on Marxist Communism (1980) 42.

Reflections on the Christian commitment to social justice.

a) Describe in your own words the "charge" that is referred to in this statement.

b) We believe in another life, a life of glory. Why is it wrong for us to ignore this world and concentrate our energies on that other, much better world?

39. Will revolution or social reform suffice to produce social justice?

Any interpretation that restricts the human predicament to a single, well-circumscribed problem, soluble through structural changes alone, is bound to be dangerously one-sided. Even to expect the solution of all human suffering or all social justice from revolution or social reform is to prepare oneself for bitter disillusionment.

U.S. Bishops, Pastoral Letter on Marxist Communism (1980) 32.

Reflections on producing social justice.

a) Why do you think the bishops say that we cannot count on just revolution or social reform if we want a just world? What else would be needed?

40. What is needed for there to be peace and justice in the world?

Whatever the progress in technology and economic life, there can be neither justice nor peace in the world, so long as men fail to realize how great is their dignity; for they have been created by God and are His children.

Pope John XXIII, On Christianity and Social Progress (1961) 215.

Reflections on peace and justice in the world.

a) How does our failure to recognize the greatness of human dignity stand in the way of justice and peace?

b) Does the Pope say that we get our dignity from what we do or from what we are? Do you agree? Why?

41. What is the relationship between love and justice?

Christian love of neighbor and justice cannot be separated. For love implies an absolute demand for justice, namely a recognition of the dignity and rights of one's neighbor. Justice attains its inner fullness only in love. Because every man is truly a visible image of the invisible God and a brother of Christ, the Christian finds in every man God himself and God's absolute demand for justice and love.

Synod of Bishops, Justice in the World (1971) 34.

Reflections on love and justice.

a) What does it mean to say that love of neighbor and justice cannot be separated?
b) Do you agree that they cannot be separated?

42. Why is action on behalf of justice more important than technical advances?

A man is more precious for what he is than for what he has. Similarly, all that men do to obtain greater justice, wider brotherhood, and a more humane ordering of social relationships has greater worth than technical advances. For these advances can supply the material for human progress, but of themselves alone they can never actually bring it about.

Vatican II, Church in the Modern World (1965) 35.

Reflections on justice vs. technical progress.

a) The statement says that justice, brotherhood, and social ordering are more important than technical progress. What reason does Vatican II give for making this statement?
b) Do you agree with the statement? Why?

43. What do Christians believe is the essential key to a more just world?

We know as Christians that the most effective response to the ills of the world is ours to make, the duty to seek justice and equality resides with each of us. Here, in the painfully slow changing of our own lives and in the agony of living out our vocations, lies the essential key to a more decent and more human world.

U.S. Bishops, To Do the Work of Justice (1978) 47.

Reflections on the essential key to a more just world.

a) What do the bishops mean when they say that "the duty to seek justice and equality resides with each of us"?

b) How do the bishops suggest we go about performing this duty?

44. Why must the Church be concerned about justice within herself?

While the Church is bound to give witness to justice, she recognizes that anyone who ventures to speak to people about justice must first be just in their eyes. Hence we must undertake an examination of the modes of acting and of the possessions and lifestyle within the Church herself.

Synod of Bishops, Justice in the World (1971) 40.

Reflections on justice within the Church.

a) Describe in your own words the reason for the necessity for justice within the Church.

b) From what you know about the Church, is internal justice a problem for the Church?

2

Economic Justice

45. What is the Christian perspective on economic life?

Every perspective on economic life that is human, moral, and
Christian must be shaped by three questions: What does the
economy do *for* people? What does it do *to* people? And how
do people *participate* in it?

                              U.S. Bishops, Economic Justice for All (1986) 1.

Reflections on the Christian perspective on economic life.

a) What should economic life focus on?
b) Do you think the focus of the American economy is more on
people or more on things?
c) Can a businessperson or politician strive after an economy
that is both 'strong and vigorous' and 'human, moral, and
Christian,' or must he strive after one or the other?

46. What is the fundamental moral criterion for all economic decisions, policies, and institutions?

> The fundamental moral criterion for all economic decisions, policies, and institutions is this: They must be at the service of all people, especially the poor.
>
> *U.S. Bishops, Economic Justice for All (1986) 24.*

Reflections on the fundamental moral criterion for economic activity.

a) Give an example of an economic decision. An economic policy. An economic institution.

b) Why must they serve all people, and not just some people?

c) Why must they be of special service to the poor?

47. What are the moral dimensions of economic life based on?

> The basis for all that the Church believes about the moral dimensions of economic life is its vision of the transcendent worth—the sacredness—of human beings. The dignity of the human person, realized in community with others, is the criterion against which all aspects of economic life must be measured.
>
> *U.S. Bishops, Economic Justice for All (1986) 28.*

Reflections on the basis for economic morality.

a) Do you believe that there is a moral dimension to economic life? Why?

b) Do you know enough about the Soviet economy to tell whether it respects the dignity of the human person? What about the South African economy? the Brazilian economy? the U.S. economy?

c) What are some ways in which an economy might show lack of respect for the dignity of the human person?

48. What are some of the basic principles of economic life?

Catholic teaching on economic issues flows from the Church's commitment to human rights and human dignity. This living tradition articulates a number of principles which are useful in evaluating our current economic situation. Without attempting to set down an all-inclusive list, we draw the following principles from the social teachings of the Church and ask that policymakers and citizens ponder their implications. (a) Economic activity should be governed by justice and be carried out within the limits of morality. It must serve the people's needs. (b) The right to have a share of earthly goods sufficient for oneself and one's family belongs to everyone. (c) Economic prosperity is to be assessed not so much from the sum total of goods and wealth possessed as from the distribution of goods according to norms of justice. (d) Opportunities to work must be provided for those who are able and willing to work. Every person has the right to useful employment, to just wages, and to adequate assistance in case of real need. (e) Economic development must not be left to the sole judgment of a few persons or groups possessing excessive economic power, or to the political community alone. On the contrary, at every level the largest possible number of people should have an active share in directing that development. (f) A just and equitable system of taxation requires assessment according to ability to pay. (g) Government must play a role in the economic activity of its citizens. Indeed, it should promote in a suitable manner the production of a sufficient supply of material goods. Moreover, it should safeguard the rights of all citizens, and help them find opportunities for employment.

U.S. Bishops, The Economy: Human Dimensions (1975) 5.

Relections on the basic principles of economic life.

a) What does it mean to say that the economy should be "governed by justice"?

b) How are two economies likely to be different if one is "carried out within the limits of morality" and the other is not?

c) If EVERYONE has the right to a sufficient share of earthly goods, is it ever moral and just for a person to starve to death?

d) What about living in extreme poverty: Can it be justified or does it violate this right?

e) Two islands are each inhabited by 100 people. The economy of island A is worth $5 million; the economy of island B is worth $3 million. Island A has two millionaires and about three dozen people living in poverty. Island B has no millionaires and a few individuals living in poverty. In your opinion, which has the healthier economy?

f) Does an individual owe it to society to work? Does society owe it to an individual to make sure that he has work?

g) Answer this multiple choice question and then explain the reasons for your answer: The economy of an area should be run by (1) the elected leaders supported by the people; (2) the people supported by their elected leaders; (3) those within the area who are politically and economically strongest; (4) those within the area who have the greatest economic expertise.

h) In the previous question, what is wrong with the three answers you rejected?

i) Do you agree that a person earning $100,000 a year should pay a lot more taxes than a person earning $10,000 a year?

j) What do you think of the proposition that, when it comes to the economy, the government that governs less, governs best?

49. List six basic human rights in economic life noted by the Church in its teaching.

In its teaching, the Church has noted a number of basic human rights in economic life, including the right to productive employment, the right to just wages, the right to an adequate income, the rights of workers to organize and bargain collectively, the right to own property for the many as a protection of freedom, and the right to participation in economic decisions.

U.S. Bishops, To Do the Work of Justice (1978) 28.

Reflections on six basic human rights in economic life.

a) Give an example of the violation of the right to productive employment.

b) Give an example of the violation of the right to just wages.

c) Give an example of the violation of the right to an adequate income.

d) Give an example of the violation of the right of workers to organize and bargain collectively.

e) Give an example of the violation of the right to own property.

f) Give an example of the violation of the right to participation in economic decisions.

g) Have you had a personal experience of the violation of any of these rights? If so, describe it.

50. What are the priorities established in Catholic teaching on the economic order?

The needs of the poor take priority over the desires of the rich; the rights of workers over the maximization of profits; the preservation of the environment over uncontrolled industrial expansion; production to meet social needs over production for military purposes.

Pope John Paul II, Address on Christian Unity in a Technological Age (Toronto, Canada, 1984).

Reflections on priorities in the economic order.

a) Explain what each of these four priorities means.

b) Explain in each case the reason why the first item is of greater importance than the second item.

c) How does this statement of Pope John Paul II strike you: Does it express your feelings, or does it represent a point of view that is different from yours?

51. Do individuals have a right to private property?

The right of private property, including that pertaining to goods devoted to productive enterprises, is permanently valid. Indeed, it is rooted in the very nature of things, whereby we learn that individual men are prior to civil society, and hence, that civil society is to be directed toward men as its end. Indeed, the right of private individuals to act freely in economic affairs is recognized in vain, unless they are at the same time given an opportunity of freely selecting and using things necessary for the exercise of this right.

Pope John XXIII, On Christianity and Social Progress (1961) 109.

Reflections on the right to private property.

a) There seem to be two basic justifications for private property given in this statement. Can you point them out?

b) Basing your explanation on the above statement, tell what happens to an individual when his/her right to ownership is denied.

52. Is private property an absolute right?

Private ownership confers on no one a supreme and unconditional right. No one is allowed to set aside solely for his own advantage possessions which exceed his needs when others lack the necessities of life.

Pope Paul VI, On the Development of Peoples (1967) 23.

Christian tradition has never upheld this right (to ownership) as absolute and untouchable. On the contrary, it has always understood this right within the broader context of the right common to all to use the goods of the whole of creation: The right to private property is subordinated to the right to common use, to the fact that goods are meant for everyone.

Pope John Paul II, On Human Work (1981) 14.

No one can ever own capital resources absolutely or control their use without regard for others and society as a whole. This applies first of all to land and natural resources. Short-term profits reaped at the cost of depletion of natural resources or the pollution of the environment violate this trust.

U.S. Bishops, Economic Justice for All (1986) 112.

Reflections on private property as an absolute right.

a) Explain in your own words what it means to say that the right to private property is not absolute.

b) Restate Pope Paul's second sentence in your own words and explain what sounds right or wrong about it.

c) What does Pope Paul seem to be saying to an extremely rich person living in our society?

d) The American bishops bring up the issue of the misuse of natural resources. What does this have to do with private property?

e) What does Pope John Paul mean by "the right to common use"?

53. What does it mean to say that we are trustees of God's creation?

Our faith teaches us that 'the earth is the Lord's' (Ps 24) and that wealth and private property are held in trust for others. We are trustees of God's creation, and as good stewards we are required to exercise that trust for the common good and benefit of our brothers and sisters.

U.S. Bishops, The Right to a Decent Home (1975) 10.

Reflections on trusteeship of God's creation.

a) Using something you own in your explanation, tell what it means to hold private property in trust for others.

b) Do you agree with the notion that I should use my personal belongings not just for my good but for the common good, and not just for my benefit but for the benefit of my fellow human beings? Why?

54. How does the Church view the pursuit of possessions?

An evergrowing supply of possessions is not to be so highly valued either by nations or by individuals as to be considered the ultimate goal. For all development has a twofold effect: on the one hand it is necessary for man so that he develop himself as a human being more and more, on the other it imprisons him as it were if it is sought as the highest good beyond which one is not to look. When this takes place hearts are hardened, minds are closed, men unite not to foster friendship but to gain advantage and as a consequence easily fall into opposition and disunity. Consequently the exclusive quest for economic possessions not only impedes man's development as a human being but also opposes his true greatness. For both nations and men who are infected with the vice of avarice give clearest evidence of moral underdevelopment.

Pope Paul VI, On the Development of Peoples (1967) 19.

Reflections on the pursuit of possessions.

a) According to this statement, our ultimate goal is not to own more and more things. Do you agree or disagree? Why?

b) "All development has a twofold effect," in other words, bettering yourself economically is a legitimate human goal, and yet it brings problems with it. What is the bright side of bettering yourself financially? What is the dark side of bettering yourself financially?

c) Pope Paul, in a much quoted statement, refers to avarice (greed) as "evidence of moral underdevelopment." What do you suppose he meant by that?

55. Does everyone have a basic right to the necessities of life?

The right to have a share of earthly goods sufficient for oneself and one's family belongs to everyone. The Fathers and Doctors of the Church held this view, teaching that men are obliged to come to the relief of the poor, and to do so not merely out of their superfluous goods.

Vatican II, Church in the Modern World (1965) 69.

Reflections on the right to the necessities of life.

a) What right does the council say belongs to everyone? Do you agree? Why?

b) Do you agree that we have an obligation to come to the relief of the poor? Why?

c) What does it mean to say that we should help the poor "not merely out of (our) superfluous goods"?

56. What right does a person in extreme necessity have?

If a person is in extreme necessity, he has the right to take from the riches of others what he himself needs.

Vatican II, Church in the Modern World (1965) 69.

As the Roman pontiffs have repeatedly emphasized in their recent encyclicals, and as accepted Catholic morality has always taught, whenever a person or a group is deprived of its basic necessities, expropriation is justified. In such an extreme case the poor have not chosen social warfare; it is imposed upon them by the injustices of the possessors.

U.S. Bishops, Pastoral Letter on Marxist Communism (1980) 44.

Reflections on the right of a person in extreme necessity.

a) What right is expressed in both of the above statements?

b) How does each statement express the condition under which the right exists?

c) Some people would say that it sounds like stealing to them. Obviously the Catholic bishops of the United States and the world do not believe in stealing. Why do you think they would say that, under the circumstances described, it is not stealing?

57. What are those to do who have received a greater share of goods?

Whoever has received from the bounty of God a greater share of goods, whether corporeal and external, or of the soul, has received them for this purpose, namely, that he employ them for his own perfection and, likewise, as a servant of Divine Providence, for the benefit of others.

Pope Leo XIII, On the Condition of Workers (1891) 36.

Reflections on those who have more goods.

a) According to this, what is a person supposed to do if he or she has more than others? Do you agree? Why?

b) What are the two purposes in having physical and spiritual goods?

58. Is equality of income and wealth a demand of justice?

Catholic social teaching does not maintain that a flat, arithmetical equality of income and wealth is a demand of justice, but it does challenge economic arrangements that leave large numbers of people impoverished. Further, it sees extreme inequality as a threat to the solidarity of the human community, for great disparities lead to deep social divisions and conflict.

U.S. Bishops, Economic Justice for All (1986) 74.

Reflections on equality of income and wealth.

a) Does justice require that everyone have exactly the same amount of income and wealth? Why?

b) Granted that we all have different amounts of income and wealth, when do those differences become unjust?

c) Why is extreme inequality in income and wealth a serious problem in society?

59. How can you tell if a society is just or unjust?

The way society responds to the needs of the poor through its public policies is the litmus test of its justice or injustice.

U.S. Bishops, Economic Justice for All (1986) 123.

The justice of a socioeconomic system and, in each case, its just functioning, deserve in the final analysis to be evaluated by the way in which man's work is properly remunerated in the system.... A just wage is the concrete means of verifying the justice of the whole socioeconomic system and, in any case, of checking that it is functioning justly. It is not the only means of checking, but it is a particularly important one and in a sense the key means.

Pope John Paul II, On Human Work (1981) 19.

Reflections on telling if a society is just or unjust.

a) What does each statement say about how we can tell if a society is just or unjust?
b) The two answers are obviously not identical. Is there or is there not a relationship between the two answers? Explain.
c) If you had to choose one or the other, which of the two gives the best way to test the justice of a society? Explain why you chose it.
d) Based on what you know of American society, would you say that it meets the criterion of the first statement? of the second statement? Give the reasons for your decision.

60. How important is it to care for the needs of the poor?

The obligation to provide justice for all means that the poor have the single most urgent economic claim on the conscience of the nation.

U.S. Bishops, Economic Justice for All (1986) 86.

The fulfillment of the basic needs of the poor is of the highest priority. Personal decisions, policies of private and public bodies, and power relationships must all be evaluated by their effects on those who lack the minimum necessities of nutrition, housing, education, and health care. In particular, this principle recognizes that meeting fundamental human needs must come before the fulfillment of desires for luxury consumer goods, for profits not conducive to the common good, and for unnecessary military hardware.

U.S. Bishops, Economic Justice for All (1986) 90.

Decisions must be judged in light of what they do *for* the poor, what they do *to* the poor, and what they enable the poor to do *for themselves.*

U.S. Bishops, Economic Justice for All (1986) 24.

Reflections on caring for the needs of the poor.

a) Restate each of the three passages in your own words.

b) Do you agree that the most urgent moral task facing us is caring for the poor? Why?

c) Give an example of how we in our society sometimes put the desire for luxury items ahead of meeting basic human needs. Why is this wrong?

d) What is meant by "profits not conducive to the common good"? When is profit-taking wrong?

e) Give an example of doing something for the poor. Give an example of doing something to the poor. Give an example of the poor being enabled to do something for themselves.

61. What is meant by the 'preferential option for the poor'?

Such perspectives provide a basis today for what is called the 'preferential option for the poor.' Though in the Gospels and in the New Testament as a whole the offer of salvation is extended to all peoples, Jesus takes the side of those most in need, physically and spiritually. The example of Jesus poses a number of challenges to the contemporary Church. It imposes a prophetic mandate to speak for those who have no one to speak for them, to be a defender of the defenseless, who in biblical terms are the poor. It also demands a compassionate vision that enables the Church to see things from the side of the poor and powerless, and to assess lifestyle, policies, and social institutions in terms of their impact on the poor. It summons the Church also to be an instrument in assisting people to experience the liberating power of God in their own lives, so that they may respond to the Gospel in freedom and in dignity. Finally, and most radically, it calls for an emptying of self, both individually and corporately, that allows the Church to experience the power of God in the midst of poverty and powerlessness.

U.S. Bishops, Economic Justice for All (1986) 52.

Reflections on the 'preferential option for the poor.'

a) Whose side did Jesus take during his life? Why do you think he took their side? Did he care about the others?

b) What does it mean to "speak for those who have no one to speak for them"? Give an example of how this might be done.

c) What does it mean to "see things from the side of the poor"? Give an example of how this might be done.

d) How does taking a look at my lifestyle help the poor?

e) Do you agree that our society and our Church should evaluate all of their policies on the basis of their impact on the poor?

f) What do you think the bishops mean when they say that the power of God can be experienced in the midst of poverty and powerlessness? Do you agree with them? Why?

62. What obligation does the preferential option for the poor place on the more fortunate in society?

In teaching us charity, the Gospel instructs us in the preferential respect due to the poor and the special situation they have in society: the more fortunate should renounce some of their rights so as to place their goods more generously at the service of others.

Pope Paul VI, A Call to Action (1971) 23.

Reflections on the obligation of the more fortunate in society.

a) What is meant by the more fortunate renouncing some of their rights? Do you agree that that should be done? Why?

63. What is the purpose of the preferential option for the poor?

The prime purpose of this special commitment to the poor is to enable them to become active participants in the life of society. It is to enable all persons to share in and contribute to the common good.

U.S. Bishops, Economic Justice for All (1986) 88.

Reflections on the purpose of the preferential option for the poor.

a) When is a person an active participant in the life of society? Give examples.

b) When is a person not an active participant in the life of society? Give examples.

c) Give an example of something society can do to "enable" everyone to participate in society.

64. Does the preferential option for the poor pit one class against another?

The 'option for the poor' is not an adversarial slogan that pits one group or class against another. Rather it states that the deprivation and powerlessness of the poor wounds the whole community. The extent of their suffering is a measure of how far we are from being a true community of persons. These wounds will be healed only by greater solidarity with the poor and among the poor themselves.

U.S. Bishops, Economic Justice for All (1986) 88.

Reflections on the option for the poor and class warfare.

a) What do you think the bishops mean when they speak of the deprivation and powerlessness of the poor wounding the entire community? How do the poor hurt those of us who are not poor?

b) Describe the cure recommended for those wounds.

c) Do you agree that giving priority to the poor does not pit one class against another? Why?

d) In Latin America people are being killed because they try to organize the poor. Why do you think rich people tend to look on solidarity among the poor as a dangerous threat?

65. What must be done beyond the helping of the poor and the hungry?

But these appeals and projects, just as funds privately and publicly allocated, gifts, and loans are not sufficient. For it is not simply a question of eliminating hunger and reducing poverty. It is not enough to combat destitution, urgent and necessary as this is. The point at issue is the establishment of a human society in which everyone, regardless of race, religion, or nationality, can live a truly human life free from bondage imposed by men and the forces of nature not sufficiently mastered, a society in which freedom is not an empty word, and where Lazarus the poor man can sit at the same table as the rich man.
Pope Paul VI, On the Development of Peoples (1967) 47.

Reflections on going beyond helping the poor and the hungry.

a) Why is it not good enough to eliminate hunger and reduce poverty?
b) What would a society be like in which "the poor man can sit at the same table as the rich man"?
c) Do you think such a society is possible? Why?

66. Under what circumstances is private or public spending morally wrong?

While so many people are going hungry, while so many families are suffering destitution, while so many people spend their lives submerged in the darkness of ignorance, while so many schools, hospitals, homes worthy of the name, are needed, every public or private squandering, every expenditure either of nations or individuals made for the sake of pretentious parade, finally every financially depleting arms race—all these we say become a scandalous and intolerable crime. The most serious obligation enjoined on us demands that we openly denounce it.
Pope Paul VI, On the Development of Peoples (1967) 53.

Reflections on the morality of private and public spending.

a) Why is private squandering morally wrong as long as there is hunger, poverty, ignorance, and inadequate medical care?

b) What is meant by "pretentious parade" on the part of individuals and nations? Why is it morally wrong as long as there is hunger, poverty, ignorance, and inadequate medical care?

c) Why is the arms race "a scandalous and intolerable crime" as long as there is hunger, poverty, ignorance, and inadequate medical care?

67. When is a productive, well-distributed economy unjust?

If the organization and structure of economic life be such that the human dignity of workers is compromised, or their sense of responsibility is weakened, or their freedom of action is removed, then we judge such an economic order to be unjust, even though it produces a vast amount of goods, whose distribution conforms to the norms of justice and equity.

Pope John XXIII, On Christianity and Social Progress (1961) 83.

Reflections on the justice of a productive, well-distributed economy.

a) What are the three circumstances under which an economy is to be judged unjust?

b) Explain why each circumstance makes an economy unjust?

68. What is the ultimate and basic purpose of economic production?

The ultimate and basic purpose of economic production does not consist merely in the increase of goods produced, nor in profit nor prestige; it is directed to the service of man, of man, that is, in his totality, taking into account his material needs and the requirements of his intellectual, moral, spiritual, and religious life; of all men whomsoever and of every group of men of whatever race or from whatever part of the world.

Vatican II, Church in the Modern World (1965) 64.

Reflections on the purpose of economic production.

a) Why can't the basic purpose of economic production be the increase of goods produced?
b) Why can't profit be the basic purpose of economic production?
c) How is economic production supposed to take into account all of our requirements: material, intellectual, etc.?
d) Why must economic production take into account the requirements of all people everywhere?

69. What does the dignity of work consist of?

(The) description of creation, which we find in the very first chapter of the Book of Genesis, is also in a sense the first 'gospel of work.' For it shows what the dignity of work consists of: It teaches that man ought to imitate God, his creator, in working, because man alone has the unique characteristic of likeness to God. Man ought to imitate God both in working and also in resting, since God himself wished to present his own creative activity under the form of work and rest.

Pope John Paul II, On Human Work (1981) 25.

Reflections on the dignity of work.

a) In what sense is work an imitation of God?
b) Why does the pope refer to Genesis as the first 'gospel of work'?
c) Is there dignity attached only to work, or is there also dignity attached to rest? Why?

70. What determines the ethical value of human work?

Human work has an ethical value of its own, which clearly and directly remains linked to the fact that the one who carries it out is a person, a conscious and free subject, that is to say, a subject that decides about himself.... The basis for determining the value of human work is not primarily the kind of work being done, but the fact that the one who is doing it is a person.

Pope John Paul II, On Human Work (1981) 6.

Reflections on the ethical value of human work.

a) The statement says that work is ethical when it is done by a free person deciding about himself. Why is it unethical when the person doing it is not free and deciding about himself?

b) Why is the person more important than the work he is doing?

71. What is the ethical meaning of work?

If one wishes to define more clearly the ethical meaning of work, it is this truth that one must particularly keep in mind. Work is a good thing for man—a good thing for his humanity—because through work man not only transforms nature, adapting it to his own needs, but he also achieves fulfillment as a human being and indeed in a sense becomes 'more a human being.'

Pope John Paul II, On Human Work (1981) 9.

Reflections on the ethical meaning of work.

a) What are the two reasons given for work being a good thing for people?

b) List several types of work with which you are familiar and explain what they have to do with transforming nature and achieving human fulfillment.

72. What is the duty to work based on?

Man must work both because the Creator has commanded it and because of his own humanity, which requires work in order to be maintained and developed. Man must work out of regard for others, especially his own family, but also for the society he belongs to, the country of which he is a child and the whole human family of which he is a member, since he is the heir to the work of generations and at the same time a sharer in building the future of those who will come after him in the succession of history. All this constitutes the moral obligation of work, understood in its wide sense.

Pope John Paul II, On Human Work (1981) 16.

Reflections on the duty to work.

a) List the four reasons given for our obligation to work.
b) What does it mean to say that we are heirs to the work of generations?
c) What does our work have to do with those who will come after us?

73. How important is work in the whole area of social justice?

Human work is a key, probably the essential key, to the whole social question, if we try to see that question really from the point of view of man's good. And if the solution—or rather the gradual solution—of the social question, which keeps coming up and becomes ever more complex, must be sought in the direction of 'making life more human,' then the key, namely human work, acquires fundamental and decisive importance.
Pope John Paul II, On Human Work (1981) 3.

Reflections on work in the area of social justice.

a) What do you think the pope meant by "the social question"?
b) Why would work be the key to the solution of "the social question"?

74. Do workers have a right to form unions?

The Church fully supports the right of workers to form unions or other associations to secure their rights to fair wages and working conditions. This is a specific application of the more general right to associate.... No one may deny the right to organize without attacking human dignity itself. Therefore, we firmly oppose organized efforts, such as those regrettably now seen in this country, to break existing unions and prevent workers from organizing.... We vehemently oppose violations of the freedom to associate, wherever they occur, for they are an intolerable attack on social solidarity.
U.S. Bishops, Economic Justice for All (1986) 104-05.

Reflections on the right to form unions.

a) Why does the Church support the right to form unions?
b) What image do you have of unions? Are they good for workers? Are they good for the country?

75. Do workers have a right to strike?

One method used by unions in pursuing the just rights of their members is the strike or work stoppage, as a kind of ultimatum to the competent bodies, especially the employers. This method is recognized by Catholic social teaching as legitimate in the proper conditions and within just limits. In this connection workers should be assured the right to strike, without being subjected to personal penal sanctions for taking part in a strike. While admitting that it is a legitimate means, we must at the same time emphasize that a strike remains, in a sense, an extreme means. It must not be abused; it must not be abused especially for 'political' purposes.

Pope John Paul II, On Human Work (1981) 20.

Reflections on the right to strike.

a) Catholic social teaching recognizes the right to strike "in the proper conditions and within just limits." What do you think would be improper conditions and unjust limits?
b) Do strikes help or hurt workers?
c) Do you agree that workers have the right to strike? Why?

76. What must be considered in determining an appropriate wage?

In determining what constitutes an appropriate wage, the following must necessarily be taken into account: first of all, the contribution of individuals to the economic effort; the economic state of the enterprises within which they work; the requirements of each community, especially as regards overall employment; finally, what concerns the common good of all peoples, namely, of the various States associated among themselves, but differing in character and extent.

Pope John XXIII, On Christianity and Social Progress (1961) 71.

Reflections on determining an appropriate wage.

a) Restate in your own words each of the four factors that should influence the determination of an appropriate wage.

b) Explain why each is a legitimate factor that should be taken into account.

c) Using these criteria, when do you think the minimum wage is just, and when is it unjust?

77. Which has priority: capital or labor?

We must first of all recall a principle that has always been taught by the church: the principle of the priority of labor over capital. This principle directly concerns the process of production: In this process labor is always a primary efficient cause, while capital, the whole collection of means of production, remains a mere instrument or instrumental cause. This principle is an evident truth that emerges from the whole of man's historical experience.... The hierarchy of values and the profound meaning of work itself require that capital should be at the service of labor and not labor at the service of capital.

Pope John Paul II, On Human Work (1981) 12, 23.

Reflections on the priority of labor over capital.

a) What does it mean to say that labor is a primary efficient cause and capital is an instrumental cause?

b) Why does labor take priority over capital?

c) Give an example of the violation of this principle.

78. What is the error of economism?

This way of stating the issue contained a fundamental error, what we can call the error of economism, that of considering human labor solely according to its economic purpose. This fundamental error of thought can and must be called an error of materialism, in that economism directly or indirectly includes a conviction of the primacy and superiority of the material, and directly or indirectly places the spiritual and the personal (man's activity, moral values and such matters) in a position of subordination to material reality.

Pope John Paul II, On Human Work (1981) 13.

Reflections on economism.

a) Why is it wrong to consider human labor solely according to its economic purpose?

b) Do you agree that the spiritual and personal are superior to the material? Why?

79. What is the church's duty regarding workers?

The church considers it her task always to call attention to the dignity and rights of those who work, to condemn situations in which that dignity and those rights are violated, and to help to guide the above-mentioned changes so as to ensure authentic progress by man and society.

Pope John Paul II, On Human Work (1981) 1.

Reflections on the church's duty regarding workers.

a) Explain how each of the tasks listed is a proper function of the church.

b) Describe a situation in which the dignity and rights of workers are violated. What would need to be done to correct the situation?

80. How important is full employment?

Full employment is the foundation of a just economy. The most urgent priority for domestic economic policy is the creation of new jobs with adequate pay and decent working conditions.

U.S. Bishops, Economic Justice for All (1986) 136.

Reflections on the importance of full employment.

a) What does it mean to say that a just economy is based on full employment? Do you agree? Why?

b) Most of us would agree that it is unrealistic to expect for

there to be 100 percent employment all the time. What is full
· employment, then, or in other words, at what point do you not
have full employment?

c) Do you agree that proper job creation is an urgent priority?
Why?

**81. Can high unemployment be tolerated in order to hold down infla-
tion?**

There are those who insist that we must tolerate high levels of
unemployment for some, in order to avoid ruinous inflation for
all. Although we are deeply concerned about inflation, we
reject such a policy as not grounded in justice.

U.S. Bishops, The Economy: Human Dimensions (1975) 14.

Reflections on unemployment vs. inflation.

a) Why would the bishops say that unemployment is a more
serious problem than inflation?

b) Do you agree with them? Why?

c) A contrary argument says that inflation is more important
because it hurts everyone while unemployment does not. Explain how unemployment hurts not just the unemployed but
everyone.

**82. What is the government's role in addressing the problem of unem-
ployment?**

Government has a prominent and indispensable role to play in
addressing the problem of unemployment. The market alone
will not automatically produce full employment. Therefore, the
government must act to ensure that this goal is achieved by co-
ordinating general economic policies, by job creation programs, and by other appropriate policy measures.

U.S. Bishops, Economic Justice for All (1986) 154.

Reflections on the government and unemployment.

a) Why won't the market alone produce full employment?
b) What are job creation programs? Many people do not think that the government should be involved in such programs. What is your opinion?

83. What is the basis for the obligation to provide unemployment benefits?

The obligation to provide unemployment benefits, that is to say, the duty to make suitable grants indispensable for the subsistence of unemployed workers and their families, is a duty springing from the fundamental principle of the moral order in this sphere, namely the principle of the common use of goods or, to put it in another and still simpler way, the right to life and subsistence.

Pope John Paul II, On Human Work (1981) 18.

Reflections on unemployment benefits.

a) Explain in your own words why workers should be given benefits while they are unemployed.
b) The pope implies that it is immoral not to help unemployed workers? Do you agree? Why?

84. Why are competition and private initiative insufficient to assure the success of development?

The initiatives of individuals and the fluctuations of competition will not assure the success of development. For it is not lawful to go to such lengths that the resources and power of the rich become even greater, and the distress of the needy be increased and the enslavement of the oppressed aggravated.

Pope Paul VI, On the Development of Peoples (1967) 33.

Reflections on competition and private initiative.

a) The statement says that it is unlawful for private initiative and competition to lead to a situation in which the rich get richer and the poor get poorer. Do you agree or disagree? Why?

b) What restrictions, if any, should be placed on private initiative?

c) What is meant by "enslavement of the oppressed"? Give examples.

85. Has the Church been critical of capitalism?

From this point of view the position of 'rigid' capitalism continues to remain unacceptable, namely the position that defends the exclusive right to private ownership of the means of production as an untouchable 'dogma' of economic life. The principle of respect for work demands that this right should undergo a constructive revision both in theory and in practice.

Pope John Paul II, On Human Work (1981) 14.

In *Quadragesimo Anno* Pope Pius XI referred to the liberal theory of uncontrolled competition as a 'poisoned spring' from which have originated all the errors of individualism. The French hierarchy, commenting upon the same pope's letter on communism, stated: 'By condemning the actions of communist parties, the Church does not support the capitalist regime. It is most necessary that it be realized that in the very essence of capitalism—that is to say, in the absolute value that it gives to property without reference to the common good or to the dignity of labor—there is a materialism rejected by Christian teaching.'

U.S. Bishops, Pastoral Letter on Marxist Communism (1980) 62.

Reflections on the church and capitalism.

a) The first statement rejects the proposition that the means of production (factories, farms, mines, etc.) should be owned exclusively by private citizens. What other kind of ownership is there? Do you agree or disagree that there should be both types of ownership? Why?

b) Why do you think the pope sees a conflict between respect for work and the exclusive right to private ownership of the means of production?

c) What do you think is meant in the second statement by un-controlled competition? When is competition in need of control?

d) Mention is made of the church's condemnation of communism. What do you think is the church's argument with communism in the area of economic justice?

e) Do people have the right to do whatever they want with their property without having to be concerned about how it affects society? Why?

f) Does a businessman have the right to run his company any way he wants without having to be concerned with how it affects the people who work for him? Why?

86. Under what conditions does Catholic social teaching allow for socialization of the means of production?

While we accept that for certain well-founded reasons exceptions can be made to the principle of private ownership—in our own time we even see that the system of 'socialized ownership' has been introduced—nevertheless the personalist argument still holds good both on the level of principles and on the practical level. If it is to be rational and fruitful, any socialization of the means of production must take this argument into consideration. Every effort must be made to ensure that in this kind of system also the human person can preserve his awareness of working 'for himself.' If this is not done, incalculable damage is inevitably done throughout the economic process, not only economic damage but first and foremost damage to man.

Pope John Paul II, On Human Work (1981) 15.

Reflections on socialization of the means of production.

a) Under what circumstances is 'socialized ownership' acceptable?

b) Do you think that there is some room for 'socialized ownership' within the framework of a capitalist system? Why?

87. Under what condition can public ownership of goods be expanded?

It is lawful for States and public corporations to expand their domain of ownership only when manifest and genuine requirements of the common good so require, and then with safeguards, lest the possession of private citizens be diminished beyond measure, or, what is worse, destroyed.
Pope John XXIII, On Christianity and Social Progress (1961) 117.

Reflections on the public ownership of goods.

a) According to this statement, what are the conditions for state ownership of property?
b) Give an example of state ownership which is in the interest of the common good.
c) Give an example of state ownership which is not in the interest of the common good.

88. What is required so that all peoples will have their right to development fulfilled?

In order that the right to development may be fulfilled by action: a) people should not be hindered from attaining development in accordance with their own culture; b) through mutual cooperation, all peoples should be able to become the principal architects of their own economic and social development; c) every people, as active and responsible members of human society, should be able to cooperate for the attainment of the common good on an equal footing with other peoples.
Synod of Bishops, Justice in the World (1971) 71.

Reflections on the right to development.

a) Pick a Third World country and restate each of these rights in terms of that country.
b) Explain why that same country has each of these three rights.

c) Explain whether you think larger countries like the United States and the Soviet Union deal with smaller countries like Nicaragua and Afghanistan "on an equal footing."

89. What is the Church's role in economic life?

It is not the Church's role to create or promote a specific new economic system. Rather, the Church must encourage all reforms that hold out hope of transforming our economic arrangements into a fuller systemic realization of the Christian moral vision. The Church must also stand ready to challenge practices and institutions that impede or carry us farther away from realizing this vision.

U.S. Bishops, Economic Justice for All (1986) 129.

Reflections on the Church's role in economic life.

a) What are the two roles outlined here for the church in the economic order? Do you consider them legitimate roles? Why?
b) Give an example of an economic practice or institution which stands in the way of the realization of the Christian moral vision.
c) Give an example of an economic reform which, in your opinion, would help realize the Christian moral vision.

90. What principles apply to the Church as economic actor?

All the moral principles that govern the just operation of any economic endeavor apply to the Church and its agencies and institutions; indeed the Church should be exemplary.

U.S. Bishops, Economic Justice for All (1986) 347.

Reflections on the Church as economic actor.

a) Why is the Church subject to the same moral principles as any other economic institution?
b) Does the Church come across to you as an example of a just economic operation? Explain.

91. What should be the Church's attitude in its use of temporal possessions?

> In regard to temporal possessions, whatever be their use, it must never happen that the evangelical witness which the Church is required to give becomes ambiguous.... Our faith demands of us a certain sparingness in use, and the Church is obliged to live and administer its own goods in such a way that the Gospel is proclaimed to the poor. If instead the Church appears to be among the rich and the powerful of this world, its credibility is diminished.
>
> *Synod of Bishops, Justice in the World (1971) 47.*

Reflections on the Church's use of temporal possessions.

a) What is meant by "a certain sparingness in use" of goods? Do you agree that our faith demands it? Explain.

b) What does the Church's administration of its goods have to do with the proclamation of the Gospel to the poor?

c) If someone told you that it is his or her perception that the Church is "among the rich and the powerful of this world," what would be your response?

92. What questions should be asked about the lifestyle of Catholics and their Church?

> In the case of needy peoples it must be asked whether belonging to the Church places people on a rich island within an ambient of poverty. In societies enjoying a higher level of consumer spending, it must be asked whether our lifestyle exemplifies that sparingness with regard to consumption which we preach to others as necessary in order that so many millions of hungry people throughout the world may be fed.
>
> *Synod of Bishops, Justice in the World (1971) 48.*

All of us must examine our way of living in light of the needs of the poor. Christian faith and the norms of justice impose distinct limits on what we consume and how we view material goods.

U.S. Bishops, Economic Justice for All (1986) 75.

Reflections on the lifestyle of Catholics and the Catholic Church.

a) A connection is made in the first statement between our lifestyle and the fate of hungry millions. Explain that connection as you see it.

b) Do you agree that "all of us must examine our way of living in light of the needs of the poor"? Why?

c) Is limiting what we consume good for the economy? Is it just or unjust, according to the bishops? What is your opinion?

d) How are we supposed to reconcile the demands of justice with the requirements for a healthy economy?

3

Political Justice

93. What are the basic political rights of individuals?

The rights of the person require that individuals have an effective role in shaping their own destinies. They have a right to participate in the political process freely and responsibly. They have a right to free access to information, freedom of speech and press, as well as freedom of dissent. They have a right to be educated and to determine the education of their children. Individuals and groups must be secure from arrest, torture and imprisonment for political or ideological reasons, and all in society, including migrant workers, must be guaranteed juridical protection of their personal, social, cultural and political rights. *Pope Paul VI, Message Issued in Union with the Synod of Bishops (1974).*

Reflections on the basic political rights of individuals.

a) What are some ways in which one can participate in the political process?

b) Why is free access to information an important right?

c) Why is freedom of speech an important right?
d) Why is freedom of dissent an important right?
e) Why is the right to be educated listed among political rights?
f) Do you agree that individuals should not be arrested for political reasons?
g) Do you agree that migrant workers have personal, social, cultural, and political rights which should be protected? Why?

94. What rights and duties do political communities have?

Political communities have the right to existence, to self-development, and to the means necessary for this. They have the right to play the leading part in the process of their own development and the right to their good name and due honors. From which it follows at one and the same time that they have also the corresponding duty of respecting these rights in others and of avoiding acts which violate them.

Pope John XXIII, Peace on Earth (1963) 92.

Reflections on the rights and duties of political communities (states).

a) Explain what each of the following statements means:
• Every nation has the right to exist.
• Every nation has the right to self-development.
• Every nation has the right to the means for self-development.
• Every nation has the right to play the leading part in the process of its own development.
• Every nation has the right to a good name.
• Every nation has the duty to respect these rights in other nations.

b) Describe circumstances under which one or more of these rights is violated.

95. How do civil authority and its laws relate to the rights of its citizens?

In recent years there has been a growing realization throughout the world that protecting and promoting the inviolable rights of persons are essential duties of civil authority, and that the maintenance and protection of human rights are primary purposes of law.

U.S. Bishops, Pastoral Plan for Pro-life Activities (1975) 26.

Reflections on civil authority and the rights of citizens.

a) Some might say that the primary purpose of law is the maintenance of order in society. The bishops say that the primary purposes of law are the maintenance and protection of human rights. Which side do you agree with? Why?

b) Give an example of law maintaining and protecting human rights.

96. What is the moral function of government?

The teachings of the church insist that government has a moral function: protecting human rights and securing basic justice for all members of the commonwealth. Society as a whole and in all its diversity is responsible for building up the common good. But it is government's role to guarantee the minimum conditions that make this rich social activity possible, namely, human rights and justice.

U.S. Bishops, Economic Justice for All (1986) 122.

Reflections on the moral function of government.

a) The bishops refer to human rights and justice as "minimum conditions." What do they mean by that?

b) By referring to the "moral" function of government, the bishops imply that it is "immoral" for government not to protect human rights and secure basic justice for all. Do you agree with them? Why?

97. What is the proper role of government?

Government should not replace or destroy smaller communities and individual initiative. Rather it should help them to contribute more effectively to social well-being and supplement their activity when the demands of justice exceed their capacities. This does not mean, however, that the government that governs least governs best. Rather it defines good government intervention as that which truly 'helps' other social groups contribute to the common good by directing, urging, restraining, and regulating economic activity.

U.S. Bishops, Economic Justice for All (1986) 124.

Reflections on the proper role of government.

a) Give an example of what you think is government replacing or destroying individual initiative.

b) Why is it not true to say that the government that governs least governs best?

c) What are some things government can do to direct, urge, restrain, and regulate economic activity?

98. Is government the answer to all of society's problems?

The Church opposes all statist and totalitarian approaches to socioeconomic questions. Social life is richer than governmental power can encompass. All groups that compose society have responsibilities to respond to the demands of justice.

U.S. Bishops, Economic Justice for All (1986) 121.

Reflections on government and the problems of society.

a) Compare totalitarian approaches with other approaches to socioeconomic problems.

b) Give some examples of groups other than government which must respond to the demands of justice.

c) State in your own words why government is not the answer to all of society's problems.

99. What is the essential sense of the State?

The essential sense of the State, as a political community, consists in that the society and people composing it are master and sovereign of their own destiny.

Pope John Paul II, Redeemer of Man (1979) 17.

Reflections on the essential sense of the State.

a) Why is it important that people be master of their own destiny?

b) To what extent are people in a dictatorship master of their own destiny? To what extent are people in a democracy master of their own destiny?

100. When is that sense unrealized?

This sense remains unrealized if, instead of the exercise of power with the moral participation of the society or people, what we see is the imposition of power by a certain group upon all the other members of the society.

Pope John Paul II, Redeemer of Man (1979) 17.

Reflections on the sense of the State unrealized.

a) What did the pope mean when he spoke of the moral participation of the people in the exercise of power?

b) When the members of Congress pass a law and the President signs it, is that an example of a certain group imposing power on the other members of society? Why?

101. What is the principle of the 'free society'?

The usages of society are to be the usages of freedom in their full range. These require that the freedom of man be respected as far as possible, and curtailed only when and in so far as necessary.

Vatican II, Declaration on Religious Freedom (1965) 7.

Reflections on the principle of the free society.

a) Why is freedom essential to society?

b) Give an example of legitimate curtailment of freedom.

c) State in your own words the principle of the free society.

102. What two factors must be kept in balance if states are to order their affairs?

As relationships multiply between men, binding them more closely together, commonwealths will more readily and appropriately order their affairs to the extent these two factors are kept in balance: 1) the freedom of individual citizens and groups of citizens to act autonomously, while cooperating one with the other; 2) the activity of the State whereby the undertakings of private individuals and groups are suitably regulated and fostered.

Pope John XXIII, On Christianity and Social Progress (1961) 66.

Reflections on the two factors to be kept in balance by states.

a) Why is it important that individual citizens be free to act autonomously?

b) Why is it important that the state to regulate the undertakings of private individuals?

c) Why is it necessary for the state to keep these two factors in balance?

d) Give an example of a state not keeping these two factors in balance.

103. Why are all citizens equal, and what should be the result of that equality?

The members of mankind share the same basic rights and duties, as well as the same supernatural destiny. Within a country which belongs to each one, all should be equal before the law, find equal admittance to economic, cultural, civic, and social life, and benefit from a fair sharing of the nation's riches.

Pope Paul VI, A Call to Action (1971) 16.

Reflections on the equality of all citizens.

a) Explain what each of these statements means:
• We all share the same basic rights.
• We all share the same basic duties.
• We should all be equal before the law.
• We should all find equal admittance to economic life.
• We should all find equal admittance to cultural life.
• We should all find equal admittance to civic life.
• We should all find equal admittance to social life.
• We should all benefit from a fair sharing of the nation's riches.

b) Explain your sense of the situation in the United States: Does EVERY American experience equality as defined here?

104. In what way can equality before the law be misused?

If, beyond legal rules, there is really no deeper feeling of respect for and service to others, then even equality before the law can serve as an alibi for flagrant discrimination, continued exploitation, and actual contempt. Without a renewed education in solidarity, an overemphasis on equality can give rise to an individualism in which each one claims his own rights without wishing to be answerable for the common good.

Pope Paul VI, A Call to Action (1971) 23.

Reflections on the misuse of equality before the law.

a) What does Pope Paul mean by "overemphasis on equality"? What is wrong with it?
b) How can equality be used as an alibi for discrimination?
c) What is individualism? What is wrong with it?
d) Explain the relationship between claiming one's own rights and being answerable for the common good.

105. What is all law based on?

All law is ultimately based on Divine Law, and a just system of law cannot be in conflict with the law of God.

U.S. Bishops, Pastoral Plan for Pro-life Activities (1975) 26.

Reflections on the basis for law.

a) What do you understand by the Divine Law?
b) Why must a just system of law conform to the Divine Law?
c) Give an example of a law which does, and an example of a law which does not, conform to the law of God.

106. What is the relationship between law and morality?

As a human mechanism, law may not be able fully to articulate the moral imperative, but neither can legal philosophy ignore the moral order.

U.S. Bishops, Pastoral Plan for Pro-life Activities (1975) 27.

Reflections on the relationship between law and morality.

a) Why can't law fully articulate morality?
b) Why can't morality be ignored in the formulation of laws?
c) State in your own words the relationship between law and morality.

107. Are laws binding if they are contrary to the moral order? Why?

Since the right to command is required by the moral order and has its source in God, it follows that, if civil authorities legislate for or allow anything that is contrary to that order and therefore contrary to the will of God, neither the laws made nor the authorizations granted can be binding on the consciences of the citizens, since we must obey God rather than men.

Pope John XXIII, Peace on Earth (1963) 51.

Reflections on laws contrary to the moral order.

a) What does it mean to say that the right to command has its source in God?
b) Give an example of a law that you think would be contrary to the will of God. What is wrong with it? Why would it be wrong to obey that law?

c) Isn't this a dangerous principle to apply? After all, who is to say what the will of God is? Suppose a murderer believes that laws against murder are immoral, isn't he correct in disobeying them?

d) Does this principle mean that individual citizens are free to obey the laws they think are right and to disobey the laws they think are wrong?

108. Why does the Church relate positively to the political order?

As part of its mission, the Church, the People of God, is required by the Gospel and its long tradition to promote and defend human rights and dignity. This view of the Church's ministry and mission requires it to relate positively to the political order, since social injustice and the denial of human rights can often be remedied only through governmental action.

U.S. Bishops, Political Responsibility (May 1976) 3.

Reflections on the Church and the political order.

a) The bishops say that the Gospel requires the Church to defend human rights and dignity. Give an example from the life and teachings of Jesus relating to human rights and dignity.

b) Do you agree that social injustice and the denial of human rights can often be remedied only through governmental action? If you agree, give an example. If you disagree, tell why.

c) The bishops say that the Church must relate positively to the political order. That is easy to understand when the political order is a democracy. But what if the Church finds itself in a communist or military dicatorship: Must it still relate positively to the political order? Why?

109. Is the Church bound to any political system?

The role and competence of the Church being what it is, she must in no way be confused with the political community, nor bound to any political system.

Vatican II, Church in the Modern World (1965) 76.

Reflections on the Church and particular political systems.

a) Why must the Church not be bound to any political system?
b) What do you think would be the consequence if the Church ever did become bound to a particular political system?

110. What is the Church's role in the political order?

The Church's role in the political order includes the following: a) education regarding the teachings of the church and the responsibilities of the faithful; b) analysis of issues for their social and moral dimensions; c) measuring public policy against Gospel values; d) participating with other concerned parties in debate over public policy; e) speaking out with courage, skill, and concern on public issues involving human rights, social justice, and the life of the Church in society.

U.S. Bishops, Political Responsibility (Feb 1976) 11.

Reflections on the Church's role in the political order.

a) Explain what each of the following means:
• The Church educates the faithful regarding their responsibilities.
• The Church analyzes issues for their social and moral dimensions.
• The Church measures public policy against Gospel values.
• The Church participates in the debate over public policy.
• The Church speaks out on public issues involving human rights, social justice, and the life of the Church in society.
b) Do you agree that these are appropriate actions for the Church to take part in? Why?
c) Should the Church endorse specific candidates for public office? Why?

111. What are some wrong uses of power?

Power may never be used to attack the dignity of persons, to subjugate them, to prevent them from seeking and realizing the goods to which their humanity gives them a claim.

U.S. Bishops, To Live in Christ Jesus (1976) 90.

Reflections on the wrong uses of power.

a) Give an example of power being used to attack the dignity of persons.

b) Give an example of power being used to subjugate people.

c) Give an example of power being used to prevent people from realizing the goods to which they have a claim.

d) Why are these uses of power wrong?

e) Do you think power itself is good and necessary, or is it evil and unnecessary? Explain.

112. What duty do the powerful have?

The powerful have a duty to work positively for the empowerment of the weak and powerless: to help others gain control over their own lives, so that as free and responsible persons they can participate in a self-determining manner in the goods proper to human beings. The powerful must therefore work for the liberation of the oppressed and powerless.

U.S. Bishops, To Live in Christ Jesus (1976) 90-91.

Reflections on the duty of the powerful.

a) What does it mean to work for the empowerment of the weak and powerless?

b) Why do you think the bishops said that the powerful have the duty to do that?

c) Do you agree or disagree with them? Why?

d) The bishops speak first of empowerment, and then they speak of liberation. What is the relationship between the two concepts of empowerment and liberation?

113. What is the fundamental duty of power?

The fundamental duty of power is solicitude for the common good of society; this is what gives power its fundamental rights. Precisely in the name of these premises of the objective ethical order, the rights of power can only be understood on the basis of respect for the objective and inviolable rights of man.

Pope John Paul II, Redeemer of Man (1979) 17.

Reflections on the fundamental duty of power.

a) The pope makes a connection between the rights of power and the fundamental rights of people. Explain that connection.

b) The rich have economic power. Do you think rich people in general are solicitous for the common good? How might a rich person go about being solicitous for the common good?

c) Government officials have political power. Do you think that government officials in general are solicitous for the common good? How might a government official go about being solicitous for the common good?

114. Why are there many unchristian institutions in traditionally Christian nations?

Today, in traditionally Christian nations, secular institutions, although demonstrating a high degree of scientific and technical perfection and efficiency in achieving their respective ends, not infrequently are but slightly affected by Christian motivation or inspiration.... How does one explain this? It is Our opinion that the explanation is to be found in an inconsistency in their minds between religious belief and their action in the temporal sphere.

Pope John XXIII, Peace on Earth (1963) 151-52.

Reflections on unchristian institutions in Christian nations.

a) Can you think of a secular institution in our country which does not seem to be influenced much by Christianity?

b) What is the pope speaking of when he refers to an inconsistency between religious belief and action in the temporal sphere?

c) Why is such an inconsistency a problem?

115. Are some political communities superior to others?

There are no political communities which are superior by nature, and none which are inferior by nature. All political communities are of equal natural dignity, since they are bodies whose membership is made up of these same human beings.

Pope John XXIII, Peace on Earth (1963) 89.

Reflections on the equality of political communities.

a) What is the reason given for the equality of political communities?

b) Suppose one political community has a million citizens, and its neighbor has a thousand citizens. In what sense is the first political community superior, and in what sense is it not superior?

c) One political community is a democracy, and the other is a dictatorship. In what sense is the first one superior, and in what sense is it not?

d) Is this principle always acknowledged on the international scene? Give examples.

116. How does justice require us to treat other countries?

The most important duty in the realm of justice is to allow each country to promote its own development, within the framework of a cooperation free from any spirit of domination, whether economic or political.

Pope Paul VI, A Call to Action (1971) 43.

Reflections on the just treatment of other countries.

a) Why is it so important to allow each country to promote its own development?

b) Suppose a country in our part of the world wants to promote its own development in a way we do not approve of, say, through communism. Should we allow it to do so? Why?

II
Specific Areas of Social Justice

4
Discrimination

117. Are some human beings superior by nature to others?

It is not true that some human beings are by nature superior and others inferior. All men are equal in their natural dignity.
Pope John XXIII, Peace on Earth (1963) 89.

Reflections on the equality of human beings.

a) Explain the phrase "equal in their natural dignity."
b) Can you think of something that a person can do to lose his natural dignity and thus become inferior to others?

118. Why are all people equal?

Since all men possess a rational soul and are created in God's likeness, since they have the same nature and origin, have been redeemed by Christ, and enjoy the same divine calling and destiny, the basic equality of all must receive increasingly greater recognition.

Vatican II, Church in the Modern World (1965) 29.

Reflections on why all people are equal.

a) Explain what each of the following means:
• All people have a rational soul.
• All people are created in God's likeness.
• All people have the same nature.
• All people have the same origin.
• All people have been redeemed by Christ.
• All people enjoy the same divine calling and destiny.
b) Show how discrimination contradicts the above statements.

119. Why should everyone have an equal opportunity?

We are all the children of God. We share the same rights before God and man. All men of good will desire that the doors of opportunity be opened equally to all who are their brothers under our eternal Father.

U.S. Bishops, Race Relations and Poverty (1966) 8.

Reflections on equal opportunity for all.

a) According to the bishops, what is the basic reason why society should offer everyone an equal opportunity?
b) Give an example of equal opportunity being denied to each of the following: a black person, a woman, an elderly person, a handicapped person.

120. Why does the Church reject discrimination?

We cannot in truthfulness call upon that God who is the Father of all if we refuse to act in a brotherly way toward certain men, created though they be to God's image. A man's relationship with God the Father and his relationship with his brother men are so linked together that Scripture says: 'He who does not love does not know God' (1 Jn. 4:8). The ground is therefore removed from every theory or practice which leads to a distinction between men or peoples in the matter of human dignity and the rights which flow from it. As a consequence, the Church rejects, as foreign to the mind of Christ, any discrimination against men or harassment of them because of their race, color, condition of life, or religion.
Vatican II, Declaration on the Relationship of the Church to Non-Christian Religions (1965) 5.

Reflections on the rejection of discrimination.

a) What do you understand by the Biblical statement that "He who does not love does not know God"?
b) In the first sentence of this passage the Council declares that if we treat certain people badly, it will interfere with our relationship with God. Do you agree? Why?
c) Give examples of discrimination or harassment because of:
• race
• color
• condition of life
• religion
d) Discrimination is said to be "foreign to the mind of Christ." Can you think of something from the life or teachings of Christ which would indicate that he would disapprove of discrimination?

121. Why should discrimination be opposed?

There are disturbing signs of increased racial and economic segregation in urban areas. We deplore discrimination, still present in our society, against persons because of their race, economic status, sex, or religion. Such attitudes contradict the Christian belief in the equality and inherent dignity of all people and they must be opposed.

> *U.S. Bishops, The Right to a Decent Home (1975) 33.*

Reflections on opposition to discrimination.

a) The bishops saw disturbing signs of discrimination in 1975. Describe the situation as you see it at present regarding
• discrimination because of race
• discrimination because of economic status
• discrimination because of sex
• discrimination because of religion

b) Is there a contradiction between discriminating against people and being a Christian? Why?

122. What types of discrimination should be overcome and eradicated?

With respect to the fundamental rights of the person, every type of discrimination, whether social or cultural, whether based on sex, race, color, social condition, language, or religion, is to be overcome and eradicated as contrary to God's intent.

> *Vatican II, Church in the Modern World (1965) 29.*

Reflections on types of discrimination.

a) Why do you think people discriminate because of sex?
b) Why do you think people discriminate because of race?
c) Why do you think people discriminate because of social condition?
d) Why do you think people discriminate because of language?
e) Why do you think people discriminate because of religion?

123. Should affirmative action be taken to eliminate the effects of past discrimination?

Where the effects of past discrimination persist, society has the obligation to take positive steps to overcome the legacy of injustice. Judiciously administered affirmative action programs in education and employment can be important expressions of the drive for solidarity and participation that is at the heart of true justice. Social harm calls for social relief.... The nation should renew its efforts to develop effective affirmative action policies that assist those who have been excluded by racial or sexual discrimination in the past.

U.S. Bishops, Economic Justice for All (1986) 73, 167.

Reflections on affirmative action.

a) What is affirmative action?
b) What reason do the bishops give for supporting affirmative action programs?
c) Why do you think many people are opposed to affirmative action?
d) List the strengths and weaknesses of affirmative action.
e) Do you support affirmative action or are you opposed to it? Give reasons for your stand.

124. Does discrimination affect progress?

All of our strivings for true human progress will be frustrated if we cannot honestly regard each of our brothers as another self, whose true vocation, like ours, is to love and to seek and embrace the good and the true, and thus attain that higher level of life which is his destiny. This regard must be expressed also in laws and institutions.

U.S. Bishops, Human Solidarity (1970) 13.

Reflections on discrimination and progress.

a) How does discrimination frustrate our efforts at progress?
b) Why must our respect for each other be expressed in laws?

125. What is the Christian view of the differences among people?

For the Christian there is no stranger, no one so different in origin or ways that such a one can be set outside of the true human family. We accept men and women for what they are, created and redeemed by God; we accept them as they are, the product of history and culture. In them and through them, God's grace works among us.

U.S. Bishops, Cultural Pluralism in the United States (1980) 53.

Reflections on the differences among people.

a) What does it mean to say that we are "the product of history and culture"?
b) What is the difference between acknowledging our differences and discriminating?

Racial Discrimination

126. Why is racism a sin?

Racism is a sin, a sin that divides the human family, blots out the image of God among specific members of that family, and violates the fundamental human dignity of those called to be children of the same Father. Racism is the sin that says that some human beings are inherently superior and others essentially inferior because of race. It is the sin that makes racial characteristics the determining factor for the exercise of human rights. It mocks the words of Jesus: 'Treat others the way you would have them treat you.' Indeed, racism is more than a disregard for the words of Jesus; it is a denial of the truth of the dignity of each human being revealed by the mystery of the Incarnation.

U.S. Bishops, Brothers and Sisters to Us (1979) 9.

Reflections on the sin of racism.

a) List the seven things which the sin of racism does.
b) What is your definition of sin? How does racism fit that definition?
c) Why is it wrong to divide the human family?
d) Why is it wrong to use race as the basis for determining rights?

e) What is "the mystery of the Incarnation"? What does it have to do with racism?

127. Is there racism within our society and our Church?

Racism is an evil which endures in our society and in our Church. Despite apparent advances and even significant changes in the last two decades, the reality of racism remains. In large part it is only the external appearances which have changed.

U.S. Bishops, Brothers and Sisters to Us (1979) 1.

Reflections on racism in our society and our Church.

a) Racism is alleged to endure in our society. Tell why you agree or disagree.

b) Racism is alleged to endure in our Church. Tell why you agree or disagree.

c) Give examples of external appearances of racism which have changed.

128. On what basis do we judge our social structures to be racist?

The structures of our society are subtly racist, for these structures reflect the values which society upholds. They are geared to the success of the majority and the failure of the minority. Members of both groups give unwitting approval by accepting things as they are. Perhaps no single individual is to blame. The sinfulness is often anonymous but nonetheless real. The sin is social in nature in that each of us, in varying degrees, is responsible. All of us in some measure are accomplices.

U.S. Bishops, Brothers and Sisters to Us (1979) 13.

Reflections on racist social structures.

a) What do the bishops have in mind when they speak of the structures of our society?

b) What does it mean to say that those structures are "subtly racist"?

c) The bishops assert that our society makes it easier for whites to succeed and for blacks to fail. Tell why you agree or disagree with them.

d) How do we approve of the racism in our society without knowing or wanting to?

e) What is the difference between personal sin and social sin?

f) How is racism a social sin?

129. How do rights and duties relate to racial discrimination?

The conviction that all men are equal by reason of their natural dignity has been generally accepted. Hence, racial discrimination can in no way be justified, at least doctrinally or in theory. And this is of fundamental importance and significance for the formation of human society according to those principles which We have outlined above. For, if a man becomes conscious of his rights, he must become equally aware of his duties. Thus, he who possesses certain rights has likewise the duty to claim those rights as marks of his dignity, while all others have the obligation to acknowledge those rights and respect them.

Pope John XXIII, Peace on Earth (1963) 44.

Reflections on rights and duties relative to racial discrimination.

a) What does this statement say about the rights and duties of minorities?

b) What does this statement say about the rights and duties of the majority?

130. How may one's stand on affirmative action reflect racism?

Racism is sometimes apparent in the growing sentiment that too much is being given to racial minorities by way of affirmative action programs or allocations to redress long-standing imbalances in minority representation and government-funded programs for the disadvantaged. At times, protestations claiming that all persons should be treated equally reflect the desire to maintain a status quo that favors one race and social group at the expense of the poor and nonwhite.

U.S. Bishops, Brothers and Sisters to Us (1979) 18.

Reflections on racism in one's stand on affirmative action.

a) What is wrong with wanting to maintain the status quo?

b) Do you think that at times too much is given to racial minorities?

c) If you are opposed to affirmative action, what do you think should be done about the long-standing imbalances of which the bishops speak?

131. Why should American Catholics be especially sensitive to racial discrimination?

The members of every racial and ethnic group are beings of incomparable worth, yet racial antagonism and discrimination are among the most persistent and destructive evils in our nation. Those victims of discrimination of whom we are most conscious are Hispanic Americans, black Americans, and native Americans. The Catholic community should be particularly sensitive to this form of injustice because it, too, has experienced prejudice and discrimination in America based on national origin and religion.

U.S. Bishops, To Live in Christ Jesus (1976) 70.

Reflections on American Catholics and racial discrimination.

a) Tell what you know about discrimination against Catholics in American history.

b) What connection do the bishops make between that part of the American past and the racial discrimination that exists today?

132. Why is racism in our Church a serious matter?

How great is that sin of racism which weakens the Church's witness as the universal sign of unity among all peoples! How great the scandal given by racist Catholics who would make the body of Christ, the Church, a sign of racial oppression! Yet all too often the Church in our country has been for many a 'white Church,' a racist institution. Each of us as Catholics must acknowledge a share in the mistakes and sins of the past. Many of us have been prisoners of fear and prejudice. We have preached the Gospel while closing our eyes to the racism it condemns. We have allowed conformity to social pressure to replace compliance with social justice.

U.S. Bishops, Brothers and Sisters to Us (1979) 31-32.

Reflections on racism in the Church.

a) What are two reasons why racism in the Church is particularly sinful?

b) Have you seen signs of the Church in America being a 'white Church,' a racist institution?

c) When is conformity to social pressure wrong?

d) Consider the case of a Catholic who is not prejudiced and has never done anything to harm minorities. The bishops say that that Catholic "must acknowledge a share in the mistakes and sins of the past." Tell why you agree or disagree with them.

133. How should the Church combat racism?

The moral and doctrinal heresy called 'racism' works through people and through institutions. The Church's efforts must be two-pronged: directed at both 'personal racism'—combatting it in the minds and hearts of its largely white membership—and at 'institutional racism,' cleansing its institutions and organizational life.

U.S. Bishops, The Church's Response to the Urban Crisis (1968).

Reflections on the Church combatting racism.

a) What is a heresy? Why do the bishops refer to racism as a "doctrinal heresy"?

b) What is the distinction made by the bishops between personal racism and institutional racism? Why are they both wrong? Why must they both be attacked?

134. In view of the racial makeup of the world, what principles should govern our relationship to other nations?

As it happens, most of the rich, consuming nations are white and Christian; most of the world's poor are of other races and religions. Concerning our relationship to other nations, our Christian faith suggests several principles. First, racial differences should not interfere with our dealing justly and peacefully with all other nations. Secondly, those nations which possess more of the world's riches must, in justice, share with those who are in serious need. Finally, the private sector should be aware of its responsibility to promote racial justice, not subordination or exploitation, to promote genuine development in poor societies, not mere consumerism and materialism.

U.S. Bishops, Brothers and Sisters to Us (1979) 57-58.

Reflections on our relationship to other nations.

a) State briefly the three principles that should govern our relationship to other nations.
b) Do you agree that our nation must, in justice, share with those who are in serious need? Do you think we are sharing as much as we should?
c) How can the private sector promote racial justice?

Discrimination Against Women

135. Why is discrimination based on sex unjust?

Discrimination based on sex, because it radically undermines the personal identity of both women and men, constitutes a grave injustice in our society.

U.S. Bishops, To Do the Work of Justice (1978) 35.

Reflections on the injustice of discrimination based on sex.

a) Explain in your own words why sex discrimination is unjust.
b) How does sex discrimination undermine the personal identity of women?

c) How does sex discrimination undermine the personal identity of men?

136. How should we characterize the attitude that women are inferior to men?

Even today some still consider women to be men's inferiors, almost their property. It is un-Christian and inhuman for husbands to regard their wives this way; they ought instead to 'love (them) as Christ loved the Church' (Eph 5:25).

U.S. Bishops, To Live in Christ Jesus (1976) 67.

Reflections on the attitude that women are inferior to men.

a) Why is it un-Christian for husbands to consider their wives inferior to them?

b) Why is it inhuman for husbands to consider their wives inferior to them?

c) How did Christ love the Church? Why is that love a good model for the love that a husband ought to have for his wife?

137. What change is taking place in the area of women in society?

It is obvious to everyone that women are now taking part in public life. This is happening more rapidly perhaps in nations with a Christian tradition, and more slowly, but broadly, among peoples who have inherited other traditions or cultures. Since women are becoming ever more conscious of their human dignity, they will not tolerate being treated as inanimate objects or mere instruments, but claim, both in domestic and in public life, the rights and duties that befit a human person.

Pope John XXIII, Peace on Earth (1963) 41.

Reflections on the changing place of women in society.

a) Describe in your own words the change that is taking place in the area of women in society.

b) What rights and duties are women claiming in domestic life?

c) What rights and duties are women claiming in public life?

d) Why do you think the rise in women's consciousness of their rights is taking place more rapidly in nations with a Christian tradition?

138. What is a false view of the liberation of women?

Efforts to win recognition that women have the same dignity and fundamental rights as men are praiseworthy and good. But the same cannot be said of views which would ignore or deny significant differences between the sexes, undermine marriage and motherhood, and erode family life and the bases of society itself. Liberation does not lie in espousing new modes of dehumanization, nor in enslavement to an ideology which ignores the facts of human sexuality and the requirements of human dignity.

U.S. Bishops, To Live in Christ Jesus (1976) 68.

Reflections on a false view of the liberation of women.

a) The bishops speak of "significant differences between the sexes." In what ways are males and females significantly different? In what ways are they not significantly different?

b) How can efforts to win recognition for women's rights undermine marriage and motherhood?

c) What is meant by saying that "liberation does not lie in espousing new modes of dehumanization"?

139. What are the conditions for the true advancement of women?

It is a fact that in many societies women work in nearly every sector of life. But it is fitting that they should be able to fulfill their tasks in accordance with their own nature, without being discriminated against and without being excluded from jobs for which they are capable, but also without lack of respect for their family aspirations and for their specific role in contributing, together with men, to the good of society. The true advancement of women requires that labor should be structured in such a way that women do not have to pay for their advancement by abandoning what is specific to them and at the expense of the family, in which women as mothers have an irreplaceable role.

Pope John Paul II, On Human Work (1981) 19.

Reflections on the conditions for the true advancement of women.

a) What is the specific role of women in contributing to the good of society?

b) Do you think that in our society the "irreplaceable role" of women as mothers is an obstacle to their advancement?

c) Tell why you agree or disagree with the conditions laid down in this statement for the true advancement of women.

140. How should the Church relate to the movement for women's rights?

At this point in history, marked, as Pope John indicated in *Pacem in Terris*, by the growing struggle of women to achieve full development, it is urgent that the Church give tangible evidence of its commitment to the rights of women, affirming their dignity as persons, and promoting their expanded participation in ecclesial and civic life.

U.S. Bishops, To Do the Work of Justice (1978) 35.

Reflections on the Church and the movement for women's rights.

a) State in your own words what the Church's attitude to the women's rights movement should be.

b) What is your experience of the actual attitude of the Church to women and their rights?

Discrimination Against the Aged

141. What are we doing when we reject the elderly?

In rejecting the elderly, we do more than perpetuate injustice: When we reject any stage of human life, we are in effect rejecting a part of ourselves and our connections with the human community. Perhaps we react to the elderly as we do because they are an unwanted reminder of our own mortality.

U.S. Bishops, Society and the Aged (1976) 5.

Reflections on rejection of the elderly.

a) Why is it wrong to reject the elderly?
b) What do the bishops suggest as the cause of our rejection of the elderly?

142. What are the basic rights being denied many elderly people?

A brief look at the plight of many elderly people shows that they are in fact being denied (these basic) rights: a) the right to life; b) the right to a decent home; c) the right to a job; d) the right to health care; e) the right to eat; f) the right to a decent income; g) the right to equal treatment.

U.S. Bishops, Society and the Aged (1976) 10-35.

Reflections on the basic rights denied the elderly.

a) Show how many elderly people are denied each of these rights:
• the right to life
• the right to a decent home
• the right to a job
• the right to health care
• the right to eat
• the right to a decent income
• the right to equal treatment

143. Why must we speak out on behalf of the elderly?

We must raise our voices clearly and effectively as advocates for the elderly on public policy matters. Elderly people cannot compete with well-financed interest groups for national resources; like other basically powerless groups, the elderly stand to lose the most in times of economic crisis.

U.S. Bishops, Society and the Aged (1976) 50.

Reflections on speaking out on behalf of the elderly.

a) Why do the elderly stand to lose the most in times of economic crisis?

b) Give examples of ways in which public policy affects the lives of elderly people.

Discrimination Against the Handicapped

144. Why is discrimination against the handicapped wrong?

The disabled person is one of us and participates fully in the same humanity that we possess. It would be radically unworthy of man, and a denial of our common humanity, to admit to the life of the community, and thus admit to work, only those who are fully functional. To do so would be to practice a serious form of discrimination, that of the strong and healthy against the weak and sick.

Pope John Paul II, On Human Work (1981) 22.

Reflections on discrimination against the handicapped.

a) Why are the handicapped equal to the rest of us?
b) Why is it wrong to deny them admittance to the life of the community?
c) When the strong and healthy deny rights to the weak and sick, why is it a serious form of discrimination?

145. Does discrimination against the handicapped tend to be conscious and deliberate?

Few of us would admit to being prejudiced against handicapped people. We bear these people no ill will and do not knowingly seek to abrogate their rights. Yet handicapped people are visibly, sometimes bluntly different from the 'norm,' and we react to this difference. Even if we do not look down upon handicapped people, we tend all too often to think of them as somehow apart—not fully 'one of us.'

U.S. Bishops, Pastoral Statement on the Handicapped (1978).

Reflections on our attitude toward the handicapped.

a) What handicapped people have you known in your life? How "different" were they? How did people react to that difference? Were they looked down upon? Were they fully accepted, or were they thought of as somehow apart?

146. What rights of the handicapped need defense?

Defense of the right to life implies the defense of other rights which enable the handicapped individual to achieve the fullest measure of personal development of which he or she is capable. These include the right to equal opportunity in education, in employment, in housing, as well as the right to free access to public accommodations, facilities and services. Those who must be institutionalized deserve decent, personalized care and human support as well as the pastoral services of the Christian community.

U.S. Bishops, Pastoral Statement on the Handicapped (1978).

Reflections on the defense of the rights of the handicapped.

a) Tell what society can do to defend each of the following rights of the handicapped:
• the right to equal opportunity in education
• the right to equal opportunity in employment
• the right to equal opportunity in housing
• the right to free access to public places
• the right to decent, personalized care for those who must be institutionalized
• the right to the pastoral services of the Christian community

147. What do the handicapped contribute to the church?

The leaders and the general membership of the church must educate themselves to appreciate fully the contribution handicapped people can make to the church's spiritual life. Handicapped individuals bring with them a special insight into the meaning of life; for they live, more than the rest of us perhaps, in the shadow of the cross. And out of their experience they forge virtues like courage, patience, perseverance, compassion and sensitivity that should serve as an inspiration to all Christians.

U.S. Bishops, Pastoral Statement on the Handicapped (1978).

Reflections on the contribution of the handicapped to the church.

a) Why is it important to have in our community people who "live in the shadow of the cross"?

b) How do handicapped people exhibit each of the following virtues: courage, patience, perseverance, compassion, sensitivity?

Anti-Semitism

148. Are Jews to be blamed for what happened to Christ?

True, authorities of the Jews and those who followed their lead pressed for the death of Christ (cf. Jn. 19:6); still, what happened in His passion cannot be blamed upon all the Jews then living, without distinction, nor upon the Jews of today. Although the Church is the new people of God, the Jews should not be presented as repudiated or cursed by God, as if such views followed from the holy Scriptures.

Vatican II, Declaration on the Relationship of the Church to Non-Christian Religions (1965) 4.

Reflections on the Jews and the death of Christ.

a) What would you say to someone who accused the Jews of being Christ-killers?

b) When Christ established the church as the new people of God, did he reject the Jews?

c) Why do you think some Christians continue to look on Jews as inferior to them?

149. What stand does the Church take toward anti-Semitism?

The Church repudiates all persecutions against any man. Moreover, mindful of her common patrimony with the Jews, and motivated by the gospel's spiritual love and by no political considerations, she deplores the hatred, persecutions, and displays of anti-Semitism directed against the Jews at any time and from any source.

Declaration on the Relationship of the Church to Non-Christian Religions (1965) 4.

Reflections on the Church and anti-Semitism.

a) Why does the Church reject anti-Semitism?

b) What is meant by the Church's "common patrimony with the Jews"?

c) The Holocaust, that horrible act of genocide resulting in the death of some six million Jews, took place in a Christian nation. What do you think we can do as Christians to insure that such an abomination never occurs again?

5

War and Peace

150. What is the Catholic attitude toward war?

The Church's teaching on war and peace establishes a strong presumption against war which is binding on all.

U.S. Bishops, The Challenge of Peace (1983) 70.

War is the most barbarous and least effective way of resolving conflicts.

Pope John Paul II, 1982 World Day of Peace Message.

The Church cannot accept violence, especially the force of arms—which is uncontrollable once it is let loose—and indiscriminate death as the path to liberation, because she knows that violence always provokes violence and irresistibly engenders new forms of oppression and enslavement which are often harder to bear than those from which they claimed to bring freedom.

Pope Paul VI, On Evangelization in the Modern World (1975) 37.

No more war, war never again! Peace, it is peace which must guide the destinies of people and of all mankind.
Pope Paul VI, Address to the United Nations General Assembly (1965) 5.

We call in season and out of season for the international community to turn from war and to do the works of peace. The primary obligation of the nuclear age is to banish resort-to-force from the daily affairs of nations and peoples. From Pius XII to John Paul II the cry of the Church and the prayer of all believers is a reiteration of the words of Paul VI: 'No more war, war never again!' This must remain our primary response to war today.
U.S. Bishops, Statement on Registration and Conscription for Military Service (1980) 3.

Reflections on the Catholic attitude toward war.

a) What does the phrase "presumption against war" mean?
b) Why is it binding on everyone?
c) Why is war the least effective way of resolving conflicts?
d) Give an example of violence provoking violence. How does this principle apply to war?
e) When Paul VI declared "No more war, war never again," do you think he really believed that there would never be another war? If not, then why did he make the statement? Why must his statement, according to the U.S. bishops, be our primary response to war today?

f) What do you think the bishops had in mind when they called on the international community "to do the works of peace"?

151. Is counter population warfare acceptable?

Any act of war aimed indiscriminately at the destruction of entire cities or extensive areas along with their population is a crime against God and man himself. It merits unequivocal and unhesitating condemnation.
Vatican II, Church in the Modern World (1965) 80.

Not even by the broadest definition can one rationally consider combatants entire classes of human beings such as school children, hospital patients, the elderly, the ill, the average industrial worker producing goods not directly related to military purposes, farmers and many others. They may never be directly attacked.

U.S. Bishops, The Challenge of Peace (1983) 108.

Under no circumstances may nuclear weapons or other instruments of mass slaughter be used for the purpose of destroying population centers or other predominantly civilian targets.

U.S. Bishops, The Challenge of Peace (1983) 147.

Reflections on counter population warfare.

a) Why is the destruction of entire cities to be condemned?
b) If we are not allowed to destroy cities, how are we to defend ourselves against an enemy that has decided to attempt to destroy our cities?

152. Is total war acceptable?

Response to aggression must not exceed the nature of the aggression. To destroy civilization as we know it by waging a 'total war' as today it could be waged would be a monstrously disproportionate response to aggression on the part of any nation. Moreover, the lives of innocent persons may never be taken directly, regardless of the purpose alleged for doing so. To wage truly 'total' war is by definition to take huge numbers of innocent lives. Just response to aggression must be discriminate; it must be directed against unjust aggressors, not against innocent people caught up in a war not of their making.

U.S. Bishops, The Challenge of Peace (1983) 103-04.

Reflections on total war.

a) Total war is one in which everything and everyone in the enemy country becomes a potential target, and the goal of the war is to destroy everything and everyone in its path. Why is this kind of war a "disproportionate response to aggression"?

b) What does it mean to say that a just response to aggression must be discriminate?

c) Is total war the only kind that can be waged today, or is there an alternative that avoids the moral pitfalls of total war?

153. What is the Catholic attitude toward nuclear war?

Traditionally, the Church's moral teaching sought first to prevent war and then to limit its consequences if it occurred. Today the possibilities for placing political and moral limits on nuclear war are so minimal that the moral task, like the medical, is prevention: as a people, we must refuse to legitimate the idea of nuclear war.

U.S. Bishops, The Challenge of Peace (1983) 131.

Our 'no' to nuclear war must, in the end, be definitive and decisive.

U.S. Bishops, The Challenge of Peace (1983) 138.

Reflections on nuclear war.

a) Why must we say 'no' to nuclear war?

b) What does it mean to "legitimate the idea of nuclear war"? What do people do who want to refuse to legitimate the idea of nuclear war?

154. Is nuclear deterrence an acceptable policy?

In current conditions 'deterrence' based on balance, certainly not as an end in itself but as a step on the way toward a progressive disarmament, may still be judged morally acceptable. Nonetheless in order to ensure peace, it is indispensable not to be satisfied with this minimum which is always susceptible to the real danger of explosion.

Pope John Paul II, Message to the U.N. Special Session (1982) 3.

(1) If nuclear deterrence exists only to prevent the use of nuclear weapns by others, then proposals to go beyond this to planning for prolonged periods of repeated nuclear strikes and counter-strikes, or 'prevailing' in nuclear war, are not accept-

able.... (2) If nuclear deterrence is our goal, 'sufficiency' to deter is an adequate strategy; the quest for nuclear superiority must be rejected. (3) Nuclear deterrence should be used as a step on the way toward progressive disarmament. Each proposed addition to our strategic system or change in strategic doctrine must be assessed precisely in light of whether it will render steps toward 'progressive disarmament' more or less likely.

U.S. Bishops, The Challenge of Peace *(1983) 188.*

Reflections on deterrence.

a) When is nuclear deterrence considered morally acceptable?
b) Why is it wrong to plan for prolonged nuclear war?
c) Why is it wrong to count on winning a nuclear war?
d) What is the difference between the two strategies of nuclear sufficiency and nuclear superiority? Why is sufficiency acceptable and superiority unacceptable?
e) What is your view of the U.S. policy of deterrence: Does it conform to the conditions stated by the bishops?

155. Is it ever morally acceptable for a country to make the first strike in a nuclear war?

We do not perceive any situation in which the deliberate initiation of nuclear warfare on however restricted a scale can be morally justified. Non-nuclear attacks by another state must be resisted by other than nuclear means.

U.S. Bishops, The Challenge of Peace *(1983) 150.*

Reflections on a nuclear first strike.

a) Why would it be wrong for us to start a nuclear war?
b) Suppose we were losing a nonnuclear war: Would it be acceptable for us to introduce nuclear weapons in an attempt to turn the war around? Why?

156. Why is the arms race immoral?

The arms race is a threat to man's highest good, which is life; it makes poor peoples and individuals yet more miserable, while making richer those already powerful; it creates a continuous danger of conflagration, and in the case of nuclear arms, it threatens to destroy all life from the face of the earth.

Synod of Bishops, Justice in the World (1971) 9.

The arms race is an utterly treacherous trap for humanity, and one which ensnares the poor to an intolerable degree.

Vatican II, Church in the Modern World (1965) 81.

The arms race is to be condemned as a danger, an act of aggression against the poor, and a folly which does not provide the security it promises.

U.S. Bishops, The Challenge of Peace (1983) 128.

Reflections on the arms race.

a) Describe how the arms race does each of the following:
• It threatens man's highest good, which is life.
• It makes poor peoples and individuals yet more miserable; it ensnares the poor to an intolerable degree; it is an act of aggression against the poor.
• It makes richer those already powerful.
• It creates a continuous danger of conflagration.
• It threatens, in the case of nuclear arms, to destroy all life from the face of the earth.
• It is a folly which does not provide the security if promises.

157. May governments defend their people against unjust aggression?

The Council and the popes have stated clearly that governments threatened by armed, unjust aggression must defend their people. This includes defense by armed force if necessary as a last resort.

U.S. Bishops, The Challenge of Peace (1983) 75.

Reflections on defense against unjust aggression.

a) Why is defense against unjust aggression necessary?
b) What does the phrase "as a last resort" add to the statement?

158. Why and when is recourse to war permissible?

a) Just Cause: War is permissible only to confront 'a real and certain danger,' i.e., to protect innocent life, to preserve conditions necessary for decent human existence, and to secure basic human rights.... b) Competent Authority:... war must be declared by those with responsibility for public order, not by private groups or individuals.... c) Comparative Justice:... In essence: which side is sufficiently 'right' in a dispute, and are the values at stake critical enough to override the presumption against war?.... d) Right Intention:...war can be legitimately intended only for the reasons set forth above as a just cause.... e) Last Resort: For resort to war to be justified, all peaceful alternatives must have been exhausted.... f) Probability of Success: This is a difficult criterion to apply, but its purpose is to prevent irrational resort to force or hopeless resistance when the outcome of either will clearly be disproportionate or futile.... g) Proportionality:... the damage to be inflicted and the costs incurred by war must be proportionate to the good expected by taking up arms.

U.S. Bishops, The Challenge of Peace (1983) 85-99.

Reflections on the just war theory.

a) State in your own words each of the seven conditions that must be met to have a just war.
b) Explain why each condition is necessary if the war is to be considered just.
c) Why would no nuclear war ever be able to be regarded as just?

159. How does the Church view military service?

Those who devote themselves to the military service of their country should regard themselves as the agents of security and freedom of peoples. As long as they fulfill this role properly, they are making a genuine contribution to the establishment of peace.

Vatican II, Church in the Modern World (1965) 79.

The role of Christian citizens in the armed forces is a service to the common good and an exercise of the virtue of patriotism, so long as they fulfill this role within defined moral norms.

U.S. Bishops, The Challenge of Peace (1983) 232.

Reflections on military service.

a) How do the military contribute to peace?
b) What is the significance of the phrase "as long as they fulfill this role properly"?
c) What do you understand by the virtue of patriotism?

160. How does the Church view conscientious objection?

In the light of the Gospel and from an analysis of the Church's teaching on conscience, it is clear that a Catholic can be a conscientious objector to war in general or to a particular war 'because of religious training and belief'.... As we hold individuals in high esteem who conscientiously serve in the armed forces, so also we should regard conscientious objection and selective conscientious objection as positive indicators within the Church of a sound moral awareness and respect for human life.
U.S. Bishops, Declaration on Conscientious Objection and Selective Conscientious Objection (1971).

First, we support the right of conscientious objection as a valid moral position, derived from the Gospel and Catholic teaching.... Secondly, we support the right of selective conscientious objection as a moral conclusion which can be validly derived from the classical moral teaching of just war theory.

U.S. Bishops, Statement on Registration and Conscription for Military Service (1980) 7-8.

Reflections on conscientious objection.

a) What is conscientious objection? What is selective conscientious objection?
b) Why do you think the Church has come out in support of both?
c) How does the conscientious objector demonstrate sound moral awareness?
d) How does the conscientious objector demonstrate respect for human life?
e) How is conscientious objection derived from the Gospel?
f) How is conscientious objection derived from the just war theory (cf. question 158)?

161. How does the Church view pacifism?

We cannot fail to praise those who renounce the use of violence in the vindication of their rights and who resort to methods of defense which are otherwise available to weaker parties.
Vatican II, Church in the Modern World (1965) 78.

Reflections on pacifism.

a) What is pacifism?
b) Why do you think the Church has taken a stand in support of pacifism?

162. How must a Christian react to an order for him to kill a noncombatant?

No Christian can rightfully carry out orders or policies deliberately aimed at killing noncombatants.
U.S. Bishops, The Challenge of Peace (1983) 148.

Reflections on the Christian reaction to an order to kill a noncombatant.

a) Why is a Christian not allowed to carry out an order to kill a noncombatant?

b) What is the relationship between this statement and the answer to question 107?

163. What is peace?

The true and solid peace of nations can consist, not in equality of arms, but in mutual trust alone.

Pope John XXIII, Peace on Earth (1963) 113.

Peace is not merely the absence of war; nor can it be reduced solely to the maintenance of a balance of power between enemies; nor is it brought about by dictatorship. Instead, it is rightly and appropriately called an enterprise of justice. Peace results from that order structured into human society by its divine Founder, and actualized by men as they thirst after ever greater justice.

Vatican II, Church in the Modern World (1965) 78.

Peace can refer to an individual's sense of well-being or security, or it can mean the cessation of armed hostility, producing an atmosphere in which nations can relate to each other and settle conflicts without resorting to the use of arms. For men and women of faith, peace will imply a right relationship with God, which entails forgiveness, reconciliation, and union.

U.S. Bishops, The Challenge of Peace (1983) 27.

Peace is above all a state of mind.

Pope Paul VI, World Day of Peace Message (1973).

Reflections on peace.

a) What is wrong with each of the following statements:
• Peace consists in equality of arms.
• Peace is the absence of war.
• Peace is the calm that prevails in a dictatorship.

b) Explain what each of the following means:
• Peace consists in mutual trust.
• Peace is an enterprise of justice.
• Peace is a state of mind.
c) What does it mean to say that peace implies a right relationship with God?

164. What is the relationship between peace and justice?

Justice is always the foundation of peace.
U.S. Bishops, The Challenge of Peace (1983) 60.

If you want peace, work for justice.
Pope Paul VI, World Day of Peace Message, (1972).

Commitment to justice must be closely linked with commitment to peace in the modern world.
Pope John Paul II, On Human Work (1981) 2.

It does no good to work for peace as long as feelings of hostility, contempt and distrust, as well as racial hatred and unbending ideologies, continue to divide men and place them in opposing camps.
Vatican II, Church in the Modern World (1965) 82.

Reflections on the relationship between peace and justice.

a) What do you think working for justice has to do with peace?
b) What happens when we try to build peace on a foundation other than justice?

165. How are we to build up peace?

In order to build up peace the causes of discord among men, especially injustice, which foment wars, must above all be rooted out.
Vatican II, Church in the Modern World (1965) 83.

Peace is not built up only by means of politics, by the balance of forces and of interests. It is constructed with the mind, with ideas, with works of peace.

Pope Paul VI, Address to the United Nations General Assembly (1965) 5.

Reflections on building up peace.

a) What needs to be done in order to build up peace?
b) Why don't politics and the balancing of forces and interests suffice to build up peace?
c) What is meant by saying that we have to construct peace with the mind, with ideas?

166. What is the fundamental condition for peace?

These rights (of the worker) must be examined in the broad context of human rights as a whole, which are connatural with man and many of which are proclaimed by various international organizations and increasingly guaranteed by the individual states for their citizens. Respect for this broad range of human rights constitutes the fundamental condition for peace in the modern world: peace both within individual countries and societies and in international relations.

Pope John Paul II, On Human Work (1981) 16.

Reflections on the fundamental condition for peace.

a) Why is respect for human rights the fundamental condition for peace?

167. Do Christians have an obligation to work for peace?

Peacemaking is not an optional commitment. It is a requirement of our faith. We are called to be peacemakers, not by some movement of the moment, but by our Lord Jesus. The content and context of our peacemaking is set, not by some political agenda or ideological program, but by the teaching of his Church.

U.S. Bishops, The Challenge of Peace (1983) 333.

Reflections on Christians working for peace.

a) What is it about the life and teachings of Jesus that calls us to be peacemakers?

b) How do you explain the fact that there have been, and still are, wars between hostile camps of Christians?

c) How do you explain the fact that there have been, and still are, Christians who are not committed to peacemaking?

168. What is the relationship between personal sanctity and world peace?

There can be no peace between men unless there is peace within each one of them.

Pope John XXIII, Peace on Earth (1963) 165.

To have peace in our world, we must first have peace within ourselves.

U.S. Bishops, The Challenge of Peace (1983) 284.

Reflections on personal sanctity and world peace.

a) Why is peace within ourselves a necessary condition for peace in the world?

6

Capital Punishment

169. What are the values involved in the debate over capital punishment?

We should acknowledge that in the public debate over capital punishment we are dealing with values of the highest importance: respect for the sanctity of human life, the protection of human life, the preservation of order in society, and the achievement of justice through law.

U.S. Bishops, Statement on Capital Punishment (1980) 3.

Reflections on the values involved in debating capital punishment.

a) How is each of the following involved in the debate over capital punishment?
• respect for the sanctity of human life
• the protection of human life
• the preservation of order in society
• the achievement of justice through law

170. How is punishment justified?

The three justifications traditionally advanced for punishment in general are retribution, deterrence, and reform.

U.S. Bishops, Statement on Capital Punishment (1980) 4.

Reflections on the justifications for punishment.

a) What is meant by retribution as a justification for punishment? Give an example.
b) What is meant by deterrence as a justification for punishment? Give an example.
c) What is meant by reform as a justification for punishment? Give an example.

171. Can reform serve as a justification for capital punishment?

Reform or rehabilitation of the criminal cannot serve as a justification for capital punishment, which necessarily deprives the criminal of the opportunity to develop a new way of life that conforms to the norms of society and that contributes to the common good.

U.S. Bishops, Statement on Capital Punishment (1980) 5.

Reflections on reform as a justification for capital punishment.

a) Why is it impossible to use reform as a justification for capital punishment?
b) What methods of punishment would promote reform of the criminal?

172. Does deterrence serve as a justification for capital punishment?

Empirical studies in this area have not given conclusive evidence that would justify the imposition of the death penalty on a few individuals as a means of preventing others from committing crimes. There are strong reasons to doubt that many crimes of violence are undertaken in a spirit of rational calculation which would be influenced by a remote threat of death. The small number of death sentences in relation to the number of murders also makes it seem unlikely that the threat will be carried out and so undercuts the effectiveness of the deterrent.

U.S. Bishops, Statement on Capital Punishment (1980) 6.

Reflections on deterrence as a justification for capital punishment.

a) The bishops list three reasons for rejecting deterrence as a justification for capital punishment. State each in your own words.

b) The bishops assert that many crimes of violence are committed without thinking about the consequences. Do you agree? What does that have to do with capital punishment?

c) One of the bishops' arguments is the small number of death sentences in relation to the number of murders. Would greatly increasing the number of death sentences solve the problem? What other problems might it create?

173. Does retribution justify capital punishment?

We grant that the need for retribution does indeed justify punishment..... But we maintain that this need does not require nor does it justify taking the life of the criminal, even in cases of murder.

U.S. Bishops, Statement on Capital Punishment (1980) 8.

Reflections on retribution as a justification for capital punishment.

a) Why do you think some people argue in favor of capital punishment on the basis of just retribution?

b) Why do you think the bishops reject the use of capital punishment as a form of retribution?

c) Which side do you agree with? Tell why you do not accept the opposing arguments.

174. Should criminals be allowed to go unpunished?

It is morally unsatisfactory and socially destructive for criminals to go unpunished.

U.S. Bishops, Statement on Capital Punishment (1980) 8.

Reflections on the punishment of criminals.

a) Why is it wrong to let criminals go unpunished?

175. How should we determine the forms of punishment?

The forms and limits of punishment must be determined by moral objectives which go beyond the mere inflicting of injury on the guilty.... We believe that the forms of punishment must be determined with a view to the protection of society and its members and to the reformation of the criminal and his reintegration into society (which may not be possible in certain cases).

U.S. Bishops, Statement on Capital Punishment (1980) 8.

Reflections on the forms of punishment.

a) What are the two criteria to be used in determining the forms of punishment?
b) Tell why you think both criteria should be used in determining the forms of punishment.
c) What are some of the reasons why it may not be possible in certain cases to reform the criminal?

176. What difficulties are inherent in capital punishment?

With respect to the difficulties inherent in capital punishment, we note first that infliction of the death penalty extinguishes possibilities for reform and rehabilitation for the person executed as well as the opportunity for the criminal to make some creative compensation for the evil he or she has done.... Second, the imposition of capital punishment involves the possibility of mistake.... Third, the legal imposition of capital punishment in our society involves long and unavoidable delays.... Fourth, we believe that the actual carrying out of the death penalty brings with it great and avoidable anguish for the criminal, for his family and loved ones, and for those who are called on to perform or to witness the execution.... Fifth, in the present situation of dispute over the justifiability of the death penalty and at a time when executions have been rare, executions attract enormous publicity, much of it unhealthy, and stir considerable acrimony in public discussion.... Sixth, there is widespread belief that many convicted criminals are sentenced to death in an unfair and discriminatory manner.

U.S. Bishops, Statement on Capital Punishment (1980) 14-19.

Reflections on difficulties inherent in capital punishment.

a) What is the first difficulty inherent in capital punishment? Is it an insurmountable difficulty?

b) What is the second difficulty inherent in capital punishment? Is it an insurmountable difficulty?

c) What is the third difficulty inherent in capital punishment? Is it an insurmountable difficulty?

d) What is the fourth difficulty inherent in capital punishment? Is it an insurmountable difficulty?

e) What is the fifth difficulty inherent in capital punishment? Is it as applicable now as it was in 1980?

f) What is the sixth difficulty inherent in capital punishment? Do you agree that there is discrimination in the application of the death penalty?

177. Has Catholic teaching allowed for capital punishment?

Catholic teaching has accepted the principle that the state has the right to take the life of a person guilty of an extremely serious crime, and that the state may take appropriate measures to protect itself and its citizens from grave harm.... We recognize that many citizens may believe that capital punishment should be maintained as an integral part of our society's response to the evils of crime, nor is this position incompatible with the Catholic tradition.

U.S. Bishops, Statement on Capital Punishment (1980) 4, 22.

Reflections on Catholic teaching on capital punishment.

a) Is capital punishment contrary to traditional Catholic teaching?

b) What has been the basis for the Catholic acceptance of capital punishment?

178. Why, then, does the Church advocate the abolition of the death penalty?

We maintain that abolition of the death penalty would promote values that are important to us as citizens and as Christians. First, abolition sends a message that we can break the cycle of violence, that we need not take life for life, that we can envisage more humane and more hopeful and effective responses to the growth of violent crime.... Second, abolition of capital punishment is also a manifestation of our belief in the unique worth and dignity of each person from the moment of conception, a creature made in the image and likeness of God.... Third, abolition of the death penalty is further testimony to our conviction, a conviction which we share with the Judaic and Islamic traditions, that God is indeed the Lord of life.... Fourth, we believe that abolition of the death penalty is most consonant with the example of Jesus, who both taught and practiced the forgiveness of injustice.

U.S. Bishops, Statement on Capital Punishment (1980) 10-13.

Reflections on the Church's stand against the death penalty.

a) What do you think of the objection that we ought to be able to find a more humane and more hopeful and effective response to violent crime?

b) What do you think of the objection that capital punishment contradicts our belief in the unique worth and dignity of each person?

c) What do you think of the objection that God is the Lord of life and that we ought not to be taking lives?

d) What do you think of the objection that the death penalty is not in line with the example of Jesus, who taught and practiced the forgiveness of injustice?

7

Abortion

179. Why is abortion an evil?

The right to life is a basic human right which should have the protection of law. Abortion is the deliberate destruction of an unborn human being and therefore violates this right.

> *U.S. Bishops, Political Responsibility (Feb 1976) 20.*

The child in the womb is human. Abortion is an unjust destruction of a human life and morally that is murder. Society has no right to destroy this life. Even the expectant mother has no such right.

> *U.S. Bishops, Declaration on Abortion (1970).*

Reflections on abortion as an evil.

a) What is the reason given for asserting that abortion is an evil?

b) Why doesn't the expectant mother have a right to destroy the life in her womb?

c) Those who support abortion tend not to want to speak of it as murder. Why do you think that is so?

180. At what point is the unborn to be considered a human person?

Conception initiates a process whose purpose is the realization of human personality. A human person, nothing more and nothing less, is always at issue once conception has taken place. We expressly repudiate any contradictory suggestion as contrary to Judaeo-Christian traditions inspired by love for life.

U.S. Bishops, Human Life in Our Day (1968).

Reflections on the unborn as a human person.

a) If one does not become a human being at conception, when does one become a human being?

b) Some people accept that a human person is at issue once conception has taken place, yet they favor abortion for what they consider overriding considerations. What are their reasons? What would you say in response to them?

181. Is abortion the mother's private business?

The assertion is made that a woman has a right not to be forced to bear a child against her will, but when a woman is already pregnant, this right must be considered in light of the child's right to life, the woman's responsibilities as its mother, and the rights and responsibilities of the child's father. The life of the unborn child is a human life. The destruction of any human life is not a private matter, but the concern of every responsible citizen.

U.S. Bishops, Statement on Abortion (1970).

Reflections on the mother and abortion.

a) Discuss abortion from the point of view of each of the following:
• the child's right to life
• the woman's responsibilities as its mother
• the rights and responsibilities of the child's father.

b) Tell why you agree or disagree that abortion is the concern of every responsible citizen.

182. How does abortion threaten all human life?

Once we allow the taking of innocent human life in the earliest stages of its development for the sake of convenience, how can we logically protect human life at any other point, once that life becomes a burden?

U.S. Bishops, Statement on Abortion (1970).

Reflections on abortion as a threat to all human life.

a) On the basis of this statement, show the connection between abortion and
• the death penalty
• the torture of political prisoners
• extreme poverty
• war.

183. What is the connection between abortion and the struggle for peace?

Abortion in particular blunts a sense of the sacredness of human life. In a society where the innocent unborn are killed wantonly, how can we expect people to feel righteous revulsion at the act or threat of killing noncombatants in war?... We must ask how long a nation willing to extend a constitutional guarantee to the 'right' to kill defenseless human beings by abortion is likely to refrain from adopting strategic warfare policies deliberately designed to kill millions of defenseless human beings, if adopting them should come to seem 'expedient.'

U.S. Bishops, The Challenge of Peace (1983) 285, 288.

Reflections on abortion and the struggle for peace.

a) What connection do the bishops make between abortion and the military stategy of our country?
b) Do you see any difference between killing innocent unborn babies and killing innocent noncombatants in a nuclear war? Do you see any similarity between the two?

184. How serious an evil does the Church consider abortion?

Abortion is and has always been considered a serious violation of God's law. Those who obtain an abortion, those who persuade others to have an abortion, and those who perform the abortion procedures are guilty of breaking God's law. Moreover, in order to emphasize the special evil of abortion, under Church law, those who undergo or perform an abortion place themselves in a state of excommunication.
U.S. Bishops, Pastoral Message of the Administrative Committee (1973).

Reflections on abortion as a serious evil.

a) Tell why you agree or disagree that abortion is a serious violation of God's law.
b) What is excommunication? Why do you think the Church excommunicates those who undergo or perform an abortion?

Bibliography

1. Abbott, Walter M., S.J., ed., "The Documents of Vatican II," Piscataway, N.J.: New Century Publishers, 1966.

2. Benestad, J. Brian and Francis J. Butler, eds., "Quest for Justice," Washington, D.C.: United States Catholic Conference, 1981.

3. Byers, David M., ed., "Justice in the Marketplace," Washington, D.C.: United States Catholic Conference, 1985.

4. National Council of Catholic Bishops, "Economic Justice for All," 1986. Also "Justice in the World," 1971, Washington D.C.: United States Catholic Conference.

5. Nolan, Hugh J., ed., "Pastoral Letters of the United States Catholic Bishops," 4 vols., Washington, D.C.: United States Catholic Conference, 1983.

6. Pope John Paul II, "Redeemer of Man," Washington, D.C.: United States Catholic Conference, 1979.

7. Pope John XXIII, "Peace on Earth," Chicago: Claretian Publications, 1967.

Index of Sources*

Second Vatican Council:

Constitution on the Church in the Modern World (1965) - 7, 8, 14, 22, 24, 30, 42, 55, 56, 68, 109, 118, 122, 151, 156, 159, 161, 163, 164, 165.

Declaration on Religious Freedom (1965) - 4, 11, 34, 35, 101.

Declaration on the Relationship of the Church to Non-Christian Religions (1965) - 120, 148, 149.

Popes:

Leo XIII, On the Condition of Workers (1891) - 57.

Pius XI, On Reconstructing the Social Order (1931) - 17.

John XXIII, On Christianity and Social Progress (1961) - 6, 40, 51, 67, 76, 87, 102.

John XXIII, Peace on Earth (1963) - 3, 13, 94, 107, 114, 115, 117, 129, 137, 163, 168.

Paul VI, Address to the United Nations General Assembly (1965) - 150, 165.

Paul VI, On the Development of Peoples (1967) - 52, 54, 65, 66, 84.

Paul VI, A Call to Action (1971) - 31, 62, 103, 104, 116.

Paul VI, World Day of Peace Message (1972) - 164.

Paul VI, World Day of Peace Message (1973) - 163.

*Numbers refer to Questions.

Paul VI, Message Issued in Union with the Synod of Bishops (1974) - 10,93.

Paul VI, On Evangelization in the Modern World (1975) - 26, 150.

John Paul II, Redeemer of Man (1979) - 99, 100, 113.

John Paul II, Address to the United Nations General Assembly (1979) - 9.

John Paul II, On Human Work (1981) - 28, 52, 59, 69, 70, 71, 72, 73, 75, 77, 78, 79, 83, 85, 86, 139, 144, 164, 166.

John Paul II, World Day of Peace Message (1982) - 150.

John Paul II, Message to the United Nations (1982) - 154.

John Paul II, Address on Christian Unity in a Technological Age (1984) - 50.

Bishops:

Synod of Bishops, Justice in the World (1971) - 23, 29, 41, 44, 88, 91, 92, 156.

U.S. Bishops, Race Relations and Poverty (1966) - 21, 119.

U.S. Bishops, Human Life in Our Day (1968) - 180.

U.S. Bishops, The Church's Response to the Urban Crisis (1968) - 133.

U.S. Bishops, Human Solidarity (1970) - 124.

U.S. Bishops, Declaration on Abortion (1970) - 179.

U.S. Bishops, Statement on Abortion (1970) - 181, 182.

U.S. Bishops, Declaration on Conscientious Objection and Selective Conscientious Objection (1971) - 160.

U.S. Bishops, Pastoral Message of the Administrative Committee (1973) - 184.

U.S. Bishops, The Eucharist and the Hungers of the Human Family (1975) - 23.

U.S. Bishops, The Economy: Human Dimensions (1975) - 48, 81.

U.S. Bishops, The Right to a Decent Home (1975) - 53, 121.

U.S. Bishops, Pastoral Plan for Pro-life Activities (1975) - 95, 105, 106.

U.S. Bishops, Political Responsibility (Feb 1976) - 15, 33, 110, 179.

U.S. Bishops, Political Responsibility (May 1976) - 108.

U.S. Bishops, To Live in Christ Jesus (1976) - 18, 25, 111, 112, 131, 136, 138.

U.S. Bishops, Resolution on the Pastoral Concern of the Church for People on the Move (1976) - 36.

U.S. Bishops, Society and the Aged: Toward Reconciliation (1976) - 141, 142, 143.

U.S. Bishops, Statement on American Indians (1977) - 37.

U.S. Bishops, To Do the Work of Justice (1978) - 1, 43, 49, 135, 140.

U.S. Bishops, Community and Crime (1978) - 19.

U.S. Bishops, Pastoral Statement on the Handicapped (1978) - 145, 146, 147.

U.S. Bishops, Brothers and Sisters to Us (1979) - 27, 126, 127, 128, 130, 132, 134.

U.S. Bishops, Pastoral Letter on Marxist Communism (1980) - 38, 39, 56, 85.

U.S. Bishops, Cultural Pluralism in the United States (1980) - 125.

U.S. Bishops, Statement on Registration and Conscription for Military Service (1980) - 150, 160.

U.S. Bishops, Statement on Capital Punishment (1980) - 169, 170, 171, 172, 173, 174, 175, 176, 177, 178.

U.S. Bishops, Health and Health Care (1981) - 16.

U.S. Bishops, The Challenge of Peace (1983) - 5, 150, 151, 152, 153, 154, 155, 156, 157, 158, 159, 162, 163, 164, 167, 168, 183.

U.S. Bishops, Economic Justice for All (1986) - 12, 20, 32, 45, 46, 47, 52, 58, 59, 60, 61, 63, 64, 74, 80, 82, 89, 90, 92, 96, 97, 98, 123.

Index of Topics

abortion- 10, 179-184
action- 15, 23, 31, 36, 42, 88, 114, 123, 130
affirmative action- 123, 130
aged, the- 19, 141, 142, 143, 151
anti-Semitism- 149
arms race- 10, 66, 156
avarice- 54

Bible- 28, 69, 148

capital- 77
capital punishment- 169-178
capitalism- 85
church- 28, 32, 36, 37, 44, 61, 79, 90, 91, 92, 108, 109, 127, 132, 133, 140, 147, 148, 150
church institutions- 29, 90, 133
church: mission- 23, 29, 30, 108
church: responsibility- 29, 33
church: role- 31, 89, 110
civil authority- 95, 107
combatants- 151
common good- 4, 11, 24, 53, 60, 63, 76, 85, 87, 88, 96, 97, 104, 113, 159, 171
communism- 21, 85
commutative justice- 2
comparative justice- 158
competition- 84, 85
conscientious objection- 160
conversion- 26
culture- 88, 125

death penalty: see capital punishment
defense- 157, 161
democracy- 21
deterrence (capital punishment)- 170, 172
deterrence (nuclear)- 154
development- 48, 84, 88, 94, 116, 134
disarmament- 154

discrimination- 104, 120, 121, 122, 123, 124, 129, 131
   sex- 121, 122, 123, 135, 139
   religious- 120, 121, 122, 131
   language- 122
   handicapped- 144, 145
   Hispanic Americans- 131
   native Americans- 131
   national origin- 131
distributive justice- 2
divine law- 30, 105, 107, 184
duties- 3, 4, 11, 13, 94, 103, 129, 137

economic activity- 48
economic affairs- 51
economic arrangements- 58, 89
economic decisions- 46, 49
economic development- 48, 88
economic institutions- 46
economic justice- 48
economic life- 40, 45, 47, 48, 49, 67, 85, 87, 89
economic order- 50, 67
economic policies- 46, 80, 82
economic power- 48
economic process- 86
economic production- 68
economic system- 89
economism- 78
education- 37, 93, 104, 110, 123, 146
elderly: see aged
employment- 48, 49, 80, 123, 146
environment- 50, 52, 53
equality- 43, 58, 88, 103, 104, 115, 117, 118, 119, 121, 125, 126, 129, 130, 142
error- 22
euthanasia- 10

family- 9, 48, 55, 66, 72, 138, 139
forgiveness- 22, 163, 178

freedom- 1, 9, 21, 23, 34, 35, 37, 49, 51, 61, 65, 67, 74, 93, 101, 102, 150

government- 48, 82, 96, 97, 98, 108, 157

handicapped- 144, 145, 146, 147
human dignity- 3, 5, 16, 22, 27, 32, 40, 41, 47, 70, 74, 108, 111, 117, 120, 121, 126, 129, 137, 138, 140
human family- 125, 126
human rights- 9, 27, 33, 37, 48, 49, 95, 96, 108, 110, 126, 158, 166
hunger- 65, 66, 92

income- 2, 49, 58, 142
individualism- 104
individuals- 6, 11, 16, 17, 51, 102
industry- 50
inflation- 81
injustice- 18, 19, 20, 29, 59, 108, 123, 131, 135, 141, 165

Jesus Christ- 3, 15, 16, 25, 27, 41, 126, 132, 167, 178
Jews- 148, 149
justice- 1, 2, 5, 12, 15, 16, 23, 24, 27, 29, 37, 40, 41, 42, 43, 44, 58, 59, 67, 73, 81, 92, 96, 97, 98, 116, 123, 134, 163, 164, 169

labor- 77, 78, 85, 139
law- 25, 95, 103, 104, 105, 106, 107, 124, 169
lifestyle- 44, 61, 92
love- 15, 22, 24, 25, 29, 41, 120, 124, 136, 149

materialism- 78, 85, 134
migrant workers- 93
military- 50, 60, 151, 159
minorities- 19, 27, 128, 130
morality- 24, 46, 47, 48, 90, 106

nationality- 65
noncombatants- 162, 183
nuclear war- 151, 153, 154, 155
nuclear superiority- 154

option for the poor: see preferential option for the poor

pacifism- 161
participation in society- 2, 9, 12, 45, 49, 63, 93, 112, 123, 140
patriotism- 159
peace- 5, 40, 150, 154, 159, 163, 164, 165, 166, 167, 168, 183
persecution- 149
person- 1, 3, 4, 5, 8, 9, 16, 20, 22, 24, 26, 34, 35, 47, 48, 56, 70, 86, 93
political communities- 94, 99, 109, 115
political order- 108, 110
poor, the- 19, 27, 36, 46, 50, 55, 56, 59, 60, 61, 62, 63, 64, 65, 84, 91, 92, 130, 134, 156
possessions- 44, 54, 91
poverty- 15, 21, 37, 61, 65, 92
power- 2, 60, 100, 111, 112, 113
preferential option for the poor- 61, 62, 63, 64
pride- 14
priorities- 50
private initiative- 84
private property- 53, 85, 86
production- 48, 50, 51, 67, 68, 77, 86
profits- 50, 60, 68
progress- 40, 42, 79, 124
prosperity- 48
punishment (criminal)- 170, 174, 175

race- 65, 68
racism- 37, 120, 121, 122, 123, 126, 127, 128, 129, 130, 131, 132, 133, 134, 164
redemption- 3, 23, 118, 125
reform (criminal)- 170, 171, 175, 176

reform (economic)- 89
reform (social)- 38, 39
religion- 65
rest- 9, 69
retribution- 170, 173
revolution- 39
rich, the- 50, 57, 65, 84, 91, 92, 134
rights- 3, 4, 9, 11, 13, 29, 41, 48,
        62, 94, 95, 103, 104, 107,
        113, 119, 122, 129, 137, 138,
        140, 142, 145, 146, 161
    to development- 88
    to life- 9, 10, 83, 142, 156, 169,
        179, 181
    to food- 9, 13, 142
    to health care- 9, 37, 142
    to rest- 9
    to the necessities of life- 55, 56,
        142
    to freedom of expression- 9, 93
    to freedom of dissent- 93
    to freedom of religion- 9, 34, 35
    to private property- 9, 49, 51, 52,
        85, 86
    to free access to information- 93
    workers'- 49, 50, 74, 75, 79, 166
    political- 93

segregation- 121
selective conscientious objection-
    160

social conditions- 16
social institutions- 6, 12, 15, 61
social justice- 1, 2, 12, 15, 23, 27,
        29, 39, 41, 42, 43, 48, 73,
        110, 132
social structures- 15, 25, 26, 128
socialization- 86, 87
state, the- 99, 100, 102
strikes- 75
subsidiarity, principle of- 17

taxation- 48
technology- 40, 42
torture- 10
truth- 31

unemployment- 81, 82, 83
unions- 74, 75

violence- 10, 150, 172, 178

wage, just- 9, 48, 49, 59, 74, 76, 80
war- 10, 150, 151, 152, 153, 154,
        155, 157, 158, 160, 163, 165,
        183
    just war- 158, 160
wealth- 2, 48, 53, 58
women- 19, 136, 137, 138, 139, 140
work- 9, 48, 69, 70, 71, 72, 73, 78,
        144
working conditions- 9, 67, 74, 80